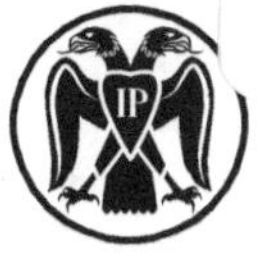

Imperium Press was founded in 2018 to supply students and laymen with works in the history of rightist thought. If these works are available at all in modern editions, they are rarely ever available in editions that place them where they belong: outside the liberal weltanschauung. Imperium Press' mission is to provide right thinkers with authoritative editions of the works that make up their own canon. These editions include introductions and commentary which place these canonical works squarely within the context of tradition, reaction, and counter-Enlightenment thought—the only context in which they can be properly understood.

HOW TO START A DISSIDENT ART MOVEMENT

ART POLEMICS 2018-2025

ALEXANDER ADAMS

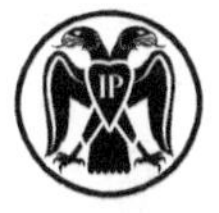

PERTH
IMPERIUM PRESS
2025

Published by Imperium Press

www.imperiumpress.org

© Alexander Adams, 2025
Used under license to Imperium Press

All rights are reserved. No part of this publication may be reproduced, stored in a retrieval system, or transmitted in any form or by any means, electronic, mechanical, photocopying, recording, or otherwise, without prior permission of Imperium Press. Enquiries concerning reproduction outside the scope of the above should be directed to Imperium Press.

FIRST EDITION

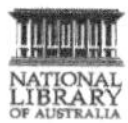

A catalogue record for this
book is available from the
National Library of Australia

ISBN 978-1-923478-24-4 Paperback
ISBN 978-1-923478-25-1 Hardcover
ISBN 978-1-923478-26-8 E-book

Imperium Press has no responsibility for the persistence or accuracy of URLs for external or third-party Internet websites referred to in this publication and does not guarantee that any content on such websites is, or will remain, accurate or appropriate.

CONTENTS

ΑΛΣ · ΙΧΗ · ΧΑΝ

INTRODUCTION

This volume contains writings about art which are of a polemical character. They form a supplement and extension to four books I published between 2019 and 2022.[1] These texts are selected, not comprehensive; excluded is the pamphlet *Abolish the Arts Council* (2022), as well as similar polemical texts dealing with art and politics. The excluded texts are largely diagnostic and seem superfluous to this collection; it is clear we have gone beyond analysis of our situation and description of the political capture of institutions. Such discussions can be found in my earlier books.

We already understand our plight; the current issue is how to overcome obstacles (external and internal) in the advancement of dissenting artists and assessment of the potential routes. When invited to speak on the parlous condition of public arts in January 2023, I chose not to enumerate faults of the Arts Council or ridicule arts programming. Instead, I announced the launch of an art movement dedicated to injecting vitality into British culture, something that nonplussed fellow panellists but en-

---

1 Namely *Culture War: Art, Identity Politics & Cultural Entryism* (Imprint Academic, 2019), *Iconoclasm, Identity Politics and the Erasure of History* (Imprint Academic, 2020), *Artivism: The Battle for Museums in the Era of Postmodernism* (Imprint Academic, 2022), *Women and Art: A Post-Feminist View* (Academica Press, 2022).

ergised the audience (which included some of the artists I had in mind).[2] Considering what is needed now, everything I selected for this book is orientated toward the future, be that making new art, overcoming challenges, setting up communities or prospering through collaboration between trusted parties (individuals, groups and companies). This collection neglects discussion of institutional decline not just because it has been done elsewhere but because it depresses and demoralises. The time for complaining is over; it holds us back.

If anyone is in need of a practical manual of how to organise a counter-cultural vanguard, this is not the book you want. It is an overview of the internal and circumstantial problems dissenting artists face, with suggestions about how to free themselves in order to make tangible progress, both personal and situational. Every artist must make his own art and the associations he forges with colleagues will be peculiar to him, his allies and the particular society he lives in (or, perhaps, the one he and his confreres will shape). I help no one by presenting plans, which must come from you and your colleagues. This book is issued to encourage readers (especially artists) to embrace bravery and optimism. You will also learn from seeing mistakes I have made along the way, both in thought and deed.

The drawback to printing older pieces is the reappearance of positions to which I no longer subscribe, as well as the presentation of arguments I would now approach differently. The pieces show my thinking evolving. This collection is an implicit invitation to consider how far you travel beside me and where you part company with me. It may be that you would not go as far as me but find the pieces worthwhile as thought experiments. Others may consider the views too moderate, damning them as warmed-over

---

2   See "The Camden Speech".

truths of a previous era. To that I demur; however, truths always bear repetition. There are always fresh ears and newly open minds ready to receive such truths.

Speculation arises in my correspondence and conversation before it appears in articles or books. One reason I have included a selection of letters in this volume is that it allows ideas to be seen in embryo form before they emerge in public form. There are other considerations which discourage articulating the truth in print. In Great Britain today there are significant costs (social, professional, financial and even legal) to opposing the status quo by expressing your values in unambiguous terms, so one has to carefully think before speaking by weighing the implications and costs of any expression. However, if one believes one has a purpose in this world – if one is convinced of the existence of souls, destinies or one's duty to kin, ancestors and common culture – then the cost of not speaking is greater than the punishment inflicted by the state or the dominant social order. Cowardice kills the heart and stifles the spirit, all the more so for being self-imposed.

Setting aside difficulties facing dissident artists in terms of making, exhibiting and selling art, that question of courage leads us to consider how we might overcome problems within ourselves. In the West, we have been raised in a world where we are taught that all peoples and cultures are equally valuable – except those of our ancestors. We are inculcated with values fundamentally untrue and unnatural; we are taught to mistrust our instincts, to ridicule the past and to passively accept the status quo as unarguably humane and enlightened when it is anything other. This plants at the core of our being a sense of shame and self-doubt (different from the Original Sin of Christian teaching) which places intolerable limits upon any man seeking to extend tradition-in-spirit rather than cling to an usurped tradition-as-form.[3] Liberation from the contemporary materialist mindset is more essential than organisational reform or countercultural resurgence, because without personal recognition of the mental schema produced within us by modern conditioning, we will perforce revert to conventional thinking. If that happens, no amount of "based patronage", independent arts bodies and dissident presses will save us.

This is a collection of discrete pieces not a unified discourse; some readers will regret the absence of argumentative connective tissue. Notes have been added only to provide references. No interpolations have been made to explain, excuse or retract points I have subsequently rejected. Texts are presented as published, with only very minor clarifying changes to punctuation or syntax. Some pieces are printed in their original long form before they were shortened for publication. With a few exceptions, pieces are arranged chronologically.

Letters and postcards collected at the conclusion of this book have been chosen on the basis that they present pithy insights, observations or surmises regarding culture. These are worth reading in conjunction with articles and books I published at the time, as they present sharper or rougher aspects of my thinking on subjects. The correspondence is not necessarily representative of the author's private writing overall but is selected because it relates to bravery and risk-taking. Another topic is mastering problems faced by artists (including the author), whether they be personal, technical, aesthetic or practical. This is the core of "Twelve Rules for Artists", which is inclusive not exclusive and comprises an outline of what I have learned. It should not be taken as a self-portrait but as an aspiration. Regrettably, I have not always lived up to the advice I have given myself

---

3   See "The Future is not Trad".

and others. If I had followed my own suggestions I should be both a better artist and a better man.

A chronology has been included. Since the first (and only previous) chronology was published in 2008, a fresh one is needed. It will help readers understand the context of articles, events and letters.

Finally, I owe an apology for too often reverting to my own work as an example of dissenting art that refuses to be either explicitly political or anti-Modernist. While I have admiration for some artists working today (as seen in the letters), I have discussed my own art rather than the art of others for a couple of reasons. Firstly, I should not claim as part of a dissenting movement art made by successful established artists, as I cannot presume to speak for those artists. I have a strong affinity with some recent art and think I understand how it operates on a level that dissenters would appreciate, but it is a step too far to appropriate it. Secondly, my own art is the art I know best and although I do not think any artist is necessarily the best arbiter of the meaning and function of his art, I think that it is a privilege he is allowed to claim. So (to put it crudely) when I say "not this way and not that way", the practising artist reading that is liable to ask "then which way?" I can offer to that artist what I have done, not because it is the solution but because it is one solution. It is down to viewer-readers to decide how far short my art falls of the heights to which I encourage others. It is for this reason I chose as the epigram for this book Jan Van Eyck's motto "ΑΛΣ · ΙΧΗ · ΧΑΝ" – "als ich kann", meaning "as I can" or "to the best of my ability".

AA, July 2025

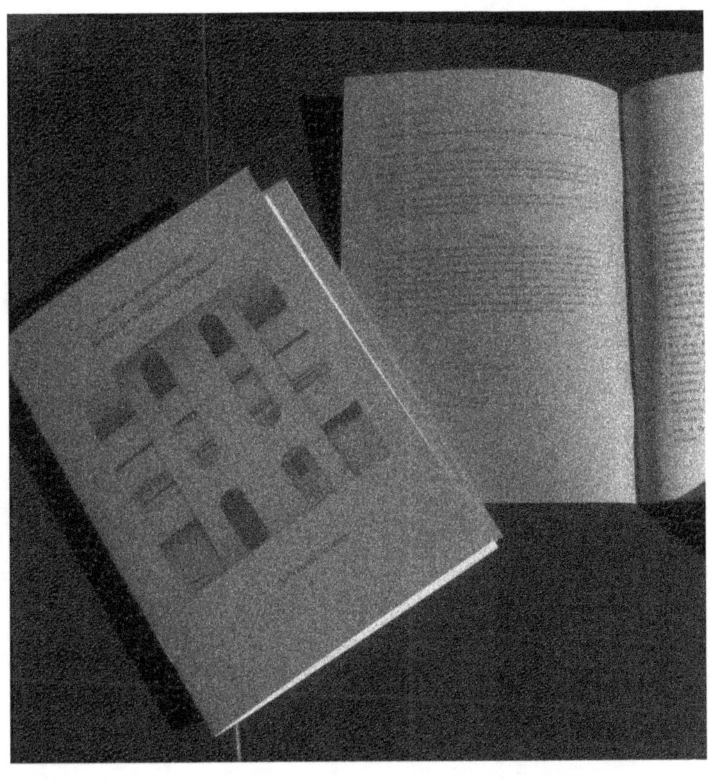

Original limited edition of *Towards a Based Barbican* (2022)

HOW TO START A DISSIDENT ART MOVEMENT

ONE

THE BARBICAN SPEECH

If you had crossed the Northern German lands in 1500, the first you would have seen of a town would have been a church spire. The church, cathedral, monastery and nunnery were concrete expressions of people's values. These buildings marked popular consent that God existed and that the institution of the church would mediate between people and God. There could have been no more stable, important and fundamental aspect in communal life than the Church. It seemed an enduring covenant.

Then in 1517 Martin Luther nailed his theses to the door of Wittenberg Cathedral and within a lifetime the Catholic Church had been practically erased from all of Northern Europe. That happened because Luther's objections reflected widespread public anger at the clergy's corruption, insularity, arrogance, hypocrisy and self-serving behaviour. The population believed in the creed and function of the Church but not its practices and personnel.

We sit today—as clergy and congregation—in one of the high cathedrals of publicly funded art. Don't assume this will last forever.

There is a gulf between the beliefs and priorities of ordinary people who fund the arts and the elite who benefit from arts funding as the primary producers, consumers and administrators of publicly funded arts. Childless individuals fund schools; healthy people fund the NHS; deaf people fund orchestras. However, what you don't find in schools, hospitals and concert halls is overt political propaganda belittling your mainstream views in favour of patriotism, Christianity, Brexit and your scepticism towards multiculturalism, transgenderism, mass migration, abortion and pushing agendas which range from the trite and self-indulgent to the patronising and demeaning. How much longer do we expect the population to fund such tendencies?

We have reached a turning point. If the publicly funded contemporary arts do not reform themselves they will be reformed—perhaps reformed out of existence. The status quo is no longer an option.

Delivered 13 October 2018, Barbican, London

TWO

———

THE CAMDEN SPEECH

We are here to discuss what to expect in the arts in the UK in 2023. In many respects, it will be grim. Prizes and media attention will be allocated according to demographic characteristics or political utility. We will see museums offloading colonial artefacts as fast as possible. Television shows and films you love will be withdrawn from circulation. Exhibitions of respected art will be turned by spiteful curators into show trials of great men. Charities will pervert the missions of museums. Publishers will fill bookshops with grievance memoirs and distorted histories and they'll all be reviewed favourably. Your culture will be traduced, your objections mocked or ignored, your efforts as makers, thinkers and lovers of the arts will be disdained. All in all, just the same as last year.

But I bring you a message of hope, one of renewal. A group of dissenting artists and makers will emerge this year, the core formed tonight, right here. They will not be driven by revenge or malice; they will not subscribe to the values of the establishment; they will work as if the people who despise their culture did not exist and treat the age in which they live in will (and must) pass before an era of true values and honest achievements (ones that our forefathers would have recognised) are restored. They will play a part in restoring those values—the supremacy of the aesthetics; striving towards beauty; dismissal of the post hoc apologia; and rejection of the state's approval. Indeed, the state's approval will become a stain, a badge of dishonour. I shan't propose a name for this movement; after all, the movements that counted most were named by those who opposed them.

Previously, I have spoken about comprehending the world through action not theory. I say we can only understand what this new movement of renewal will be by enacting it—by making, sharing, promoting, funding—and thereby come to understand what we need by seeing what we feel compelled to make. We will (consciously or otherwise) produce what is needed, what we find to be absent in the arts today. We have a deficiency in our lives, something like a vitamin deficiency, which leaves us listless, enervated, aesthetically and intellectually malnourished. This is deliberately done in the cultural field, in the same way as we are made weak and dependent on the state via medication, health advice, nudge policy and safetyism.

This renewal movement will require starting from the beginning, building a parallel economy, new channels for art, fresh systems of patronage. That is the great challenge of the year ahead. This renewal of contemporary art must be done in tandem with protecting historical collections, public statues, distinguished architecture and place names. This will be done by defunding subversion projects, abolishing the Arts Council and removing the political uniparty which keeps in place the professional management class. Regarding that, the only solution in that field is to clear them out. I commend this double mission—of renewal and defence—to you, lovers of the art here tonight.

Delivered 24 January 2023, Camden, London

THREE

THE NEW IMPRESSIONISTS

OR

HOW TO START A DISSIDENT ART MOVEMENT

When the movement we recognise under the name "the Impressionists" first exhibited together, they called the 1874 exhibition, *Société Anonyme Coopérative des Artistes Peintres, Sculpteurs, Graveurs* ("Co-operative and Anonymous Association of Painters, Sculptors and Engravers"), held at Nadar's photographic studio in Paris. They gave themselves no title, agreed no core principles, signed no manifesto. They came together in common cause in rejection of the Académie and opposition to hanging jury of the annual salon, where France's most talented professional artists exhibited, sold and were awarded prizes. Many of the exhibitors at the subsequent exhibitions had been rejected by the Académie and the salon juries, but some had not. It was Degas who insisted artists choose: henceforth they could exhibit as independents or choose the salon; they could not do both. In one respect, the motivation for the series of annual exhibitions was pragmatic or prosaic: a group of artists wanted to exhibit and sell art that official channels blocked. They wanted to advance their careers and earn money. Discrediting the state bodies was secondary; for some, perhaps it was not their intention at all, just simply an inference that others made.

When one examines the list of exhibitors at the Independent exhibitions of 1874-86, one is struck by the indisputable heterogeneity of styles, attitudes and schools. There are some artists who conventional to a T, including some sculptors of portrait busts. Some were quite established; ages spanned from the young to elderly. While all were competent, not all were original or distinguished and have lapsed into deserved obscurity. Yet, in retrospective, we separate and elevate those we call "Impressionists" because of their paintings' unfinished surfaces, rejection of the glassy varnished surfaces of the salon painters, proclivity towards the non-narrative, tendency to work plein air, painting on light grounds, committing to realism above idealism and centring petit bourgeois and working-class people as subjects for art. These shared aspects make the Impressionists stand out and retrospectively form the style of the school. The process of evolution (or at least change) was so accelerated at the time that the last exhibitions included artists such as Gauguin and Seurat who are classed as Neo-Impressionists or Post-Impressionists—the second generation of Impressionists who had developed significantly enough to be classed as successors to the exhibitions of an older generation who had started the Independent exhibitions.

What happened with the emergence of these "Impressionists" may be the case for our movement, where our style can be classed and described discretely only later, not by ourselves. It is important for us, as dissidents, to recognise that we can bond in opposition, perhaps only later coming to discern common aesthetic ideals, subjects or practices within the dissenting body. In this initial phase, it seems unwise to apply stylistic or technical criteria to those who might wish to describe themselves as part of the dissident arts movement. Yet we should retain the right to disassociate our group from any individuals or groups who claim affiliation, on the grounds that they acting contrary to intentions or good standing of our movement, with no right of appeal. A movement should be based or common benefits, experienced in shared and individual ways. Some members will gain more from collective action than others, as in true of all group activity. The group activity has meaning as an assertion of unity across one stratum, for artists who usually work and think in a solitary manner.

There are times when art is made in isolation but is seen (at a distance) to be connected. Consider the Symbolist movement. Running from the 1850s (or even the 1820s) in multiple North and Central European countries (and to a lesser extent in North America), this movement spanned continents, encompassed many distinct schools and covers artists who did not know of each other's work, yet we see many common themes. These are two examples of movements not centred on explicit creeds. The first is the Impressionists, with artists co-located in time, place and professional cognisance of their fellows but with disparate stylistic, thematic, iconographic, political and technical concerns; the second is the Symbolists, with artists generally divided by location, time and professional cognisance of their fellows but with similar stylistic, thematic, iconographic, political and technical concerns. Both are now seen as cohesive, yet at the time the artists did not (generally) link themselves formally.

We can think of the Impressionists and Symbolists as opposites to the Italian Futurists, who had a joint manifesto and committed to explicit aesthetic positions and political goals. This also applies to a slightly lesser degree to the Surrealists in Paris, organised under André Breton. Like the Futurists, they spread ideas and set an example of what was expected from group members through publications in periodicals, as well as their own journals, and newsletters. The Surrealists, who advocated psychic liberation and pursuit of the personal subconscious, were also politically orthodox Communists and prone to endless rollcalls of the faithful in terms of joint letters. The Surrealists formed groups that would examine members in hearings to determine conformity before voting on whether to expel the member. It was the worst aspects of the clique and political splinter faction.

For a new movement in our age, the Surrealist model seems the worst of all. While it led to a degree of artistic prominence and financial success for members, many of those Surrealist artists had private collectors and commercial galleries unconnected to the movement proper. The endless wrangles about who followed orthodoxy led to separate factions, such as the *Documents* group, headed by Georges Bataille. It also resulted in some of the best known Surrealists—Giacometti, Dalí, Masson—being excommunicated, with some of the best and most typical work of the school (style) being made outside the movement (organisation). This clearly damaged the credibility of the movement. The contrary peril is that careerists, opportunists and bad-faith actors take up the mantle of the dissident art movement while failing to act along the movement's main lines of artistic and political solidarity— or actually work against them. While any movement needs to possess a degree of conformity, the trials and expulsions of the Surrealist group (with endless internal drama driven by personal animus) are not feasible in an era of cancel culture. I fear that any artistic movement which relies on social media is at the mercy of drama queens, malicious individuals and tittle-tattles, seeking to use public channels of Twitter, YouTube and other social media to discredit fellow members, exclude rivals, seek popularity and spread gossip. Under such circumstances, Surrealism would have spread more widely, in terms of creators and audience, but it would have failed to maintain artistic coherence.

A protocol which might aid the dissident art movement is one that allows members to promote art and ideas through publicly visible channels but requests (and if necessary enforces) a code of silence regarding personal disagreements and individual clashes. This is difficult because artistic ideas are often deeply held by artists, in that artist and idea come to be viewed as inextricably interlinked. Generally, artists do not divorce themselves from principles or their past (or recent) work. Such breaks can be seen as admissions of failure or reversals in stance. It seems to damage the credibility of the artist and (by inference) discredit the art. So, in a movement with disagreement about artistic issues, disputes cannot help but become personal. Art history is full of such incidents and we shall be unable to avoid this path. We can help by criticising ideas and art rather than artists. Bearing those qualifications in mind, what overall principles should a successful artistic movement have?

1. Generosity. As individuals who do not believe in egalitarianism—that is to say, all are not equal nor is making all equal possible or desirable—we recognise that some of us are more skilled, more original, more powerful as artists than others. We should extend to others who share our aims and beliefs and play an active part in our community (on individual terms, by advancing our cause or by dint of their artistic contribution) a degree of generosity. In other words, we allow in those who are committed and serious, overlooking their

shortcomings as artists, while at the same time urging all to excel. This is the spirit of collegiality. We should not publicly disparage anyone who is supporting or contributing to the movement. We must act without malice.

2. Seriousness. We are serious about our principles, supporting our fellows, protecting our heritage, advancing our values, sustaining our viability. That seriousness should extend into all areas of our public conduct. That does not mean being sombre and grand and self-important, but taking our principles seriously. One means of doing so is not engaging in the trivial, of rising about banalities, be they petty personal gripes, minor matters of taste, indulging in gossip, bickering, feuding (within the movement) and being prey to the passions that the Stoics warned against. By becoming weak and failing to overcome our internal faults, we make ourselves non-serious as a movement and devalue our beliefs and our work.

3. Ambition. We need to overcome ideas, individuals and institutions that are discredited through the force of our courage and achievements. We cannot be complacent with regard to superiority over others. This means guarding against repetition, laziness and rote responses. We have to challenge ourselves to do better and constantly strive to lift ourselves and others in our movement by working harder, knowing more, sharing information (by being generous) and seeking to apply our discoveries (or rather, as perennialists, that should be "re-discoveries") to more areas.

4. Solidarity. This might also be called conformity or in-group bonding. We are aware of the tendency of those who wish to dissolve concerted opposition to use hyper-individualism as an ideal to atomise the core of

a potential rival elite. To ensure we advance our values, we expect that anyone in the movement either publicly support or not oppose those values. That can be judged through the artist's work or his public statements. The movement retains the right to disassociate itself from individuals who do not conform to this. This may or may not be made explicit publicly.

5. Quality. This is the hardest principle to enforce, as it requires a high level of discrimination, as well as personal tact and compassion. Although according to principle 1, we should welcome those makers who express solidarity and conformity, we must also exercise judgement that requires us to exclude, postpone, defer and omit. We must demand that the arts of our movement achieve a certain threshold of competency, ingenuity, truthfulness, integrity and compatibility with our values. We should not be afraid to refuse submissions to public displays or publications, while at the same time appreciating the effort and commitment of makers who currently fail to reach our standards. This may be ameliorated by having different levels of participation in public associations—for example, members, invitees and so on. We must cultivate discrimination and connoisseurship through a body of published criticism and publications which share the best art we can produce, which will help to broadcast our standards and raise the bar in terms of production.

6. Independence. The movement must resist the interference of the state and quasi-state actors, such as organisations (charities, NGOs, large corporations, lobby groups) affiliated with the state. As I discussed regarding the setting up of an arts venue, funding or representation in decision making by such bodies makes a movement vulnerable to overt leverage or co-

vert subversion.[1] Funding should ideally come through blind trusts, anonymous donations, crowd-funding and commercial activity. Large donations should come without any conditions other than providing for publications, exhibitions, documentaries etc of a high standard. We should aim to establish our own channels of dissemination wherever possible and act with generosity to allow orthodox newcomers access to these channels.

7. Authority. Our authority as leaders in a renewal of the arts depends on our exercise of the above principles, the truth of our values, our personal conduct and the high quality of our work. We need to toughen up and offer apologies only when we respect the interlocutor and recognise a genuine fault—we must never offer strategic apologies because it depletes our moral authority and the credibility of our speech. We can engage in dialogue, even when we see our interlocutor cannot be moved because it is the audience who can be persuaded in private by what he hears. If we set a moral example, then we add ethos to logos and pathos in our presentation.

This is how a movement might comport itself effectively. It says nothing about the principles or aesthetics, outside of implicit values of comportment. That will be left until later. I say nothing about the advantages and disadvantages of having a membership scheme for the movement, as that is complicated. It advantages the movement to have an inner core of an old guard, elites and decision-makers as a vanguard, and an outer group of followers, imitating, disseminating and contributing as and when they can. A thriving movement needs this separation and needs to have

1   See "Towards a Based Barbican".

a flexible and dynamic structure that allows replacement of personnel within the top cadre (the circulation of elites, as Pareto would put it), as well rewarding secondary followers and supporters.

I offer these guidelines for discussion and correction.

28 January 2023

FOUR

———

TOWARDS A BASED BARBICAN

I

When two articles by me on the subject of the Barbican Arts Centre were published in spring 2022, a number of people suggested to me that a fuller outline of the suggestions contained in those might be useful. The question that came up was, "Would a dissident arts centre be feasible?" There is an easy answer to that: yes, if permitted.

No legal contract or property deed will prevent an authority from depriving a legal owner of his rights, even if to do so laws need breaking or rewriting. Should an authority deem dissident action a threat, laws will not protect dissidents. In short, there is no law, only might. So, however diligent and judicious a plan for a dissident arts project may be, it could be dismantled by a governing power, if that power were determined enough to do so. But, should the full force of the state not be used to suppress the project, an arts venue pledged to present high-quality culture, including dissident outlooks, should be able to do more than survive, it could thrive.

Bearing that caveat in mind, it is worth exploring the idea of a dissident arts centre. This pamphlet will discuss the history of the Barbican Arts Centre in the City of London, using it as a case study of a non-state-funded arts centre. We shall look at some ways in which the Barbican has retained its independence and why—despite the possibility of it striking out in new directions and presenting a genuine counter-culture of the right—the programming of the Barbican has not strayed from the liberal/progressivist orthodoxy. We will consider ways in which a dissident arts centre may be protected from (or subverted by) the values of the governing elite. What functions could a dissident arts centre perform? Why, considering how much of a public and immobile target such an establishment would present, would we bother with such a venture? To conclude, some guiding principles are set out. A British perspective is taken but points should be applicable in any country.

By "dissident", I mean any person or group holding views roughly aligning with (or including) anti-progressivist positions that are reactionary, right wing, socially conservative, arch-traditionalist, nationalist, localist, Christian, anarchistic, libertarian or radically non-conformist. Of course, these positions are in many senses contradictory, one thing they have in common is that none will be granted a public platform, particularly in a publicly funded arts venue.[1] To be deemed a dissident all it takes (potentially) is being committed to art being judged on its intrinsic qualities and refusing to assess art according to the demographic characteristics of its maker or performer. The ranks of dissident-adjacent individuals have been swollen by large numbers of disaffected liberals and leftists who refuse to engage in identity politics. You may be a dissident without realising it. The acid-test for dissidence is being able to tolerate the existence and expression of reactionary viewpoints with which you disagree; that issue will remove

---

1   On the subject of the position of the dissident artist under a hostile governing elite, see Alexander Adams, "State Art and the Dissident Artist", *The Jackdaw*, no. 162, March/April 2022, pp. 12-3.

from the ranks of true dissidents some of those disaffected liberals and leftists, who find that they cannot accept free speech if it is used against their political values.

An arts administrator in the UK would be as likely to program a stage play—provocative but with artistic merit—that was sympathetic towards white nationalism, as he would place a live explosive in proximity to an audience, for the simple reason that dissident ideas are considered as dangerous as bombs and treated accordingly. The principle of free speech is officially upheld until someone uses it to advance ideas that undermine the beliefs of the governing elite, then community cohesion and multiculturalism trump the liberties of speaker and listeners, even those listeners who wish to understand and oppose the speaker's ideas.[2]

As I have argued elsewhere[3], supporting free speech does not mean supporting all instances with public money. Perhaps topics such as that of the notional play should be left to the private sector. Except, that should such a play ever be staged in a private venue, it would be picketed by left-wing activists, have partner companies targeted via social-media pressure, be smeared in the mainstream press, be denounced by politicians and even be suppressed by local authorities or the police on grounds of "hate speech". Ethno-nationalism—a position that every single elected politician, civil servant, media figure and arts administrator will tell you is so absurd and wrong-headed that there could not be a reasonable argument in favour of it—is too dangerous to be presented in anything other than caricatural form in an open forum, be that publicly or privately

2   See Alexander Adams, *Culture War: Art, Identity Politics and Cultural Entryism*, Imprint Academic/Societas, Exeter, 2019, pp. 27-9.
3   Alexander Adams, "Vanguards, Visions and Networks in the Arts", *Where Do We Go From Here?*, Scyldings Events, 2021, pp. 42-62.

funded. The right-thinking liberal is not sure whether white racial solidarity is so absurd it could never be taken seriously or if it is so dangerously persuasive that the whole nation (especially the working-class section) is in its thrall. To be safe, the liberal decides it is both simultaneously—[ethno-nationalism is treated as] a pathology that is both completely unjustified but frighteningly attractive, awaiting the inoculation of imposed multiculturalism. That means the arguments are too absurd to be counter-argued and too dangerous to be aired—a tactical combination that guarantees no open discussion is possible.

Lest I be accused of fabricating the chimera of political correctness as a foe in the field of culture, consider the list of serious creators whose most controversial works are now difficult (almost impossible in some cases) to discuss/display in state-funded forums: Arno Breker, William Burroughs, Louis-Ferdinand Céline, Eric Gill, Peter Handke, Martin Heidegger, H.P. Lovecraft, Graham Ovenden, Ezra Pound, Leni Riefenstahl. Even when a popular patriotic artist such as William Hogarth is exhibited, he is traduced in a show trial of progressive political morality, in an attempt to provoke, humiliate and demoralise admirers of his art.[4] The circle of unacceptable views must inevitably expand and the action against opposition will grow increasingly severe.

Make no mistake, there is no marketplace of ideas in a liberal democracy, for the public forum must be policed by right-thinkers. That means deciding that certain views are

---

4   "Hogarth and Europe" exhibition, Tate Britain, London, 2021-2; catalogue Alice Insley, Martin Myrone (eds.), *Hogarth and Europe*, Tate, London, 2021. For my discussion of the politics of the exhibition, see Adams, "Show trials of an Old Master", 8 March 2022, *Bournbrook Magazine*, https://www.bournbrookmag.com/home/shows-trials-of-an-old-master.

not only illegitimate, but that they are literally unspeakable. I may not wish to attend such a dramatic performance but I do not object to anyone writing, performing or watching such a drama. Yes, even another drama that was anti-white, although we already have plenty of public venues that host such events. I go further: I want there to be venues that might host such dramas, ones which would defend them and your right to see them. The possibility of such places coming into existence is the subject of this pamphlet.

II

My first exposure to the Barbican Arts Centre came obliquely. In the children's science-fiction drama *The Tripods*, when the producers for the (somewhat cash-strapped) BBC programme had to come up with a futuristic city-cum-biosphere in 1985, they selected the Barbican as one filming location. The palm-filled Barbican conservatory was suitably modern and exotic—at least for a child in the provinces. Years later, I worked in an office adjacent to the Barbican and walked its disorientating aerial walkways daily by rote, knowing that any clever shortcut would lead me inevitably and inconveniently astray. Barbican Library became my local library.

When it was built, between 1972 and 1982, the Barbican Arts Centre was the UK's most ambitious urban-planning project to reach construction stage. It houses cinemas, concert halls, exhibition galleries, conference rooms, a theatre, restaurants, shops, cafés, a library and car park in an estate that consists of 2,000 residences, mostly in high-rise towers, all built in a Brutalist style. The new hardback *Building Utopia: The Barbican Centre* marks the 40th anniversary of the Barbican Arts Centre's completion, the 50th anniversary of its commencement and (approximately) the 65th anniversary of its conception. Multiple specialist writers cover the origins of the project, the politics and development of the building process and outline the highlights and remit of the cultural activities of the centre. A plethora of photographs capture the centre throughout its operation, from construction up to today, with some shots of classic performances and memorable events.

The site of the Barbican Arts Centre is Aldersgate, next to Silk Street, Beech Street and Whitecross Street, close to St Paul's Cathedral in the City of London. The site had been bombed almost completely flat during the Blitz and thus the location presented itself for wholesale redevelopment—on a grand scale, integrating accommodation and facilities. It was already served by Moorgate Station (Northern line underground and mainline) and was within walking distance of the offices and banks of the City. There was little residential consultation—following wartime devastation, Cripplegate district had a residential population of 58. The photographs of the flattened district, with St Paul's in the background, is a stark reminder of the state of British cities in the post-war aftermath.

It seems the impetus behind having so many residences was partly political. Sir Nicholas Kenyon, former Managing Director of the Barbican Arts Centre, writes:

> The vanishing residential population of the Square Mile posed an existential threat to the survival of the Corporation [of the City of London], with its independent governance and long traditions, for there was a serious possibility in the post-war years that, without residents and voters, there might be a move to incorporate the City into London County Council.[5]

Hostility from LCC and the Arts Council caused friction with the Barbican and led to tussles over funding and control. LCC wanted greater commercial development; the

5   Nicholas Kenyon et al, *Building Utopia: The Barbican Centre*, Batsford, 2022, p. 31.

Corporation wanted residences and arts. The Corporation won out and architects Chamberlin, Powell and Bon were appointed to design the centre and estate buildings. An initial costing of £10m was eventually to balloon to £150m by the time of completion.

The scale of the project is still—in our age of mega-structures—impressive. ("The largest single building for the arts in the Western world."[6]) The over 30 lifts include one that can transport a 20-tonne lorry. The distinctive unpainted pitted concrete surfaces of walls were originally smooth before they were pick-hammered by men with pneumatic drills. This was time-consuming and thus expensive. Some aspects were flawed in design. The sculpture courtyard was rarely used because the weight of pieces was considered a potential structural danger to the building below. The gallery space has always been disappointing—a reflection of its late inclusion in the design—and has never lived up to the other facilities of the venue.

When the centre was opened by the Queen on 3 March 1982, the building seemed anachronistic—both behind the times and ahead of them. The building seemed ponderous and unsympathetic, alien in its stylistic unity; cultural tourism was not as developed and streamlined as it would become so there were many doubts about the viability of a costly arts hub. The architecture seemed heavy and uncompromising in a time when Post-Modernism was jettisoning concepts of "truth to materials", Brutalism and stylistic conformity. Its broad walkways and windswept courtyards seemed too ambitious and forbidding; its thick brass railings seemed passé. More than anything, Brutalism's intimidating size and lack of decorative concession seemed anti-human and indicative of failed visions of Communistic Eastern Europe and corner-cutting city councils.

6   Ibid., quoted, p. 195.

Today, attitudes to Brutalism are changing. Brutalism is an Instagram favourite topic and subject of photo essays and coffee-table books. The high aspirations and unapologetic futurity of Brutalist concrete structures exhilarates the young urban crowd.

The London Symphony Orchestra has been resident at the Barbican since it opened. The Royal Shakespeare Company acted as consultants as the theatre was designed. However, organisational politics and wrangles over income and subsidies caused Barbican to lose the RSC in an acrimonious parting in 2002. ("The RSC were reluctant tenants. We were grumpy landlords."[7]) A transcription of a discussion between senior insiders notes that "the Corporation saw the conferences as money generators, and orchestras as money spenders".[8] Balancing artistic considerations against commercial one is a constant negotiation, as is that of high culture versus experimental programming. (Although apparently the BBC-funded 1985 Stockhausen festival turned into a sell-out success.) Views on the acoustics of the concert hall were mixed; the acoustics noticeably improved once the Perspex hemispheres were removed from the ceiling. The opinions of performers, conductors and critics are summarised.

Most of the fittings are bespoke, which added to the cost but were congruent and effective within the overall design. (There is a great shot of Robin Day's strongly coloured concert-hall seats.) The signage was considered inadequate from the beginning, leading to notorious navigation difficulties. A Barbican poster announced, "If Helen Mirren can find the new Barbican Centre before it opens in March, she will be appearing in *Midsummer Night's Dream*."[9]

7   Ibid., p. 148.
8   Ibid., p. 102.
9   Ibid., quoted, p. 169.

The book has many photographs of these details, as well as plans, maps, images of construction, aerial views and vintage shots. A selection of posters show the breadth of programming over the last 40 years, reminding readers of memorable experiences. The authors are either specialists in their fields or they are individuals who have worked at a high level in the Barbican's management. Short testimonies by knowledgeable figures (including performers, managers and users) intersperse longer narratives, which show palpable affection but address faults. Subjects include the Barbican's architecture, theatre, music, art, cinema, typefaces and branding and plentiful insights into the management.

Building Utopia: The Barbican Centre presents a comprehensive and sympathetic presentation of one of modern Britain's most iconic buildings. Not universally loved as a building—indeed, still disliked by many—the Barbican continues to act as an important centre for high culture. Most importantly, the Barbican is largely an independent enterprise, with relatively low and indirect tax-payer subsidies. Today, the Barbican's distance from the interfering hand of government is more vital than ever.

III

Reviewing *Building Utopia: The Barbican Centre* caused me to return to the subject of founding dissident arts networks. Even traditional art is at this point dissident—the expression of forbidden values of family, nationalism, religious faith, aesthetic excellence and conventional beauty. Where do we go, when our museums and arts venues are in the hands of progressives who feel nothing but anger and resentment towards beautiful and illuminating art that we love? Could we set up our own Barbican Arts Centre?

In addition to the Barbican's arts programme, its functions include providing facilities for conferences, trade fairs, weddings and so on. There is an attempt to balance cultural provision with purely business services, with revenue from the latter supporting the former. Even so, the centre's management have made a point of providing serious high culture at the highest standard, especially in the field of cultural music. The inherent conservatism of the public and the appetite for popular classics is a key ingredient in programming. Consider also highly attended serious displays on modernist architecture and design, as well as exhibitions of costumes, sets and stills relating to iconic film series and directors. Not only does the centre rely on that income, it needs to retain a broad audience, cultivating an audience that attends the Barbican regularly and patronises its shops, restaurants and cafés. It cannot rely on hipsters, fashion students and trendy sociology graduates; it needs elderly ladies who listen to Handel and watch *Hamlet*. Financial imperatives remain and they direct the overall management of the centre.

The artistic programming is a mixture of events that range from the commercially viable (it hosted the initial run of *Les Miserables*) to the artistically adventurous/worthy, which are revenue negative. The income from popular mainstream events and commercial activities (supplemented by some Corporation subsidies) allows the Barbican Centre to program niche events, such as foreign film festivals, minority-creator exhibitions, politically directed displays. As the management of the Barbican is drawn from the caste of left-liberal metropolitan non-governing elite, it is to be expected it will unthinkingly transmit progressivist values. You would never encounter intellectual and political diversity outside of the annual Battle of Ideas; you would never expect a festival of feminism there to be followed by a season of reactionary literature.

The Barbican Arts Centre was established to provide arts and cultural services to the City of London and to the residents of adjoining residences. Opened in 1982, housing cinemas, theatres, galleries, library and conference rooms, the centre is owned and run by the Corporation of the City of London. It does not receive a direct grant from the Ministry of Culture (DCMS) nor Arts Council England (ACE). It is wholly owned and operated by the Corporation, funded by the income of the centre and income from the Corporation's rates, rents, fees and investment. Therefore it is—at least nominally—independent of the dread hand of DCMS and ACE and their quotas on racial equality, mandatory racial awareness training and commitments to diversity.

That is rather an academic point as—disappointingly—the Barbican is just as woke and riddled with identity politics as ACE, the Tate, the South Bank Centre and the Whitechapel Art Gallery. The important truth is not that independence from government and quangos can permit artistic freedom but that it has not resulted in that in this prominent case. The point is that there is the opportunity for the Barbican to be a force for opposition to progressivist culture, however, it has not been. Why might that be?

Individuals who manage the Barbican are no different from the staff of ACE, senior civil servants at DCMS or the directors of publicly funded venues. In fact, individuals transfer between the Barbican and these State Art bodies regularly as staff, curators and consultants, forming a vector of transmission of ideas through personnel. As the Barbican does not have an outright top-down principle of rejecting progressivism in programming, it has no resistance to the values of the governing elite coming to dominate the direction of an organisation that could (theoretically) be independent of that elite.

So, what is notable is that detachment from direct control of progressivist organisations does not automatically result in the emergence of diverse views. At the Barbican we find the same type of material we could find anywhere else in London. True, we find smaller distinguished vanguard creators given more space and funding than elsewhere, but their politics and demographic profiles are dully predictable. Now, how overrun by social justice and diversity targets the Corporation of the City of London is, I cannot say. At least a little, one must assume. Simply because the managers and directors of all major organisations are products of the last 50 years of schooling and university and tainted with the assumptions of the elite, we could not expect even an august commercially responsive organisation of today to be based, reactionary or evenly coolly mercenary.

So, the priorities of senior Barbican staff and the values of the Corporation align with the governing elite's values: multiculturalism, equality, feminism, progressivism, social justice, "diversity is our strength, comrade". Imagine if they did not. Imagine a based Barbican, where commercial activities and revenue-generating serious high culture could cross-fund festivals of Evola and Carlyle, film festivals of reactionary cinema or host an unapologetically anti-globalist drama. Imagine such events being out of the influence of ACE and DCMS, reaching not only a national but international audience. Of course, the critics of *The Guardian* would boycott performances and the BBC would casually slur (and carefully frame) this arts centre as a hotbed of bigotry. That would be precisely because there would be an obvious clash of essential values, something the governing elite could not tolerate.

We should set out the intellectual and organisational framework for such an arts venue. In practical terms, it is only by these following principles that dissident culture can establish its own arts centre which stands a chance of enduring:

(A) Dissidents must own the venue and property on which the venue is located.

(B) The organisation—at executive corporate and managerial levels—must be resistant to subversion. There should be thorough and careful scrutiny in terms of hiring, especially at upper levels. Preference should always be given to native-born individuals at senior levels. This not only encourages and rewards these individuals, it also fosters a sense that senior figures should be committed to the venue, locale and the local (or national) population rather than allowing executives to treat the venue as a node in a worldwide network of cultural venues.

(C) The venue should provide largely apolitical classic arts to a high standard and gain a reputation for reliability; this programme should be revenue neutral or revenue generating.

(D) The venue should provide more challenging programmes which reflect a genuine resistance to progressive culture and transmit reactionary/dissident values. This should involve diverse viewpoints, preferably ones that do not have an outlet elsewhere.

(E) A publishing arm should form synergies with venue-specific cultural events by cross-promoting and generating income through publishing books by/about the venue, resident performers and staff; resultant profits to be partly directed to support the venue.

(F) A cultural journal should be established, partly to promote and discuss events at the venue; it should strive to be at least revenue neutral.

(G) The venue should ideally be able to access cross-subsidisation from other commercial sources within the organisation. Note that cross-subsidisation is illegal in some contexts, so care should be taken in setting up an arrangement that might not present an easy fault line to be exploited via lawfare.

(H) The venue should not accept any government or NGO funding; it may take donations from any source with no reciprocal commitment, preferably through a blind trust; it should not endanger its independence by entering commercial partnerships that may involve any risk of political interference. In practice, any partner organisation may be pressured and steered in a way that may cause it to attempt to influence the venue, but reasonable steps should be taken to avoid such relationships. Alternative routes for banking—including crypto-currency—must be pursued to protect the venue's operations. (See point J.)

(I) The venue should host annual, biannual or triannual cultural events, encouraging and rewarding leading national practitioners in the arts, building a regular audience and increasing prestige for such events, thereby strengthening the legitimacy and appeal of these art forms for audiences, critics, patrons and creators/performers. This point is discussed in the next section.

(J) Supporters of the venue and its aims should attempt to build an alternative economy. As David Lee (among others) has documented[10], State Art maintains a largely closed economy, using public subsidies that go into state venues that advertise in state-influenced publications that review exhibitions at such venues, the venues also stocking copies of the said publication, and so on. This perpetuates a hermetic system that lacks public acclaim and appeal. Dissident artists should create their own networks, ones that retain and grow wealth within connected parts: venues, journals, books, exhibitions, artists, curators, writers, journalists, small

10   David Lee, "State Art: Safe as Houses", *The Jackdaw*, no. 162, March/April 2022, pp. 14-5.

businesses, audiences, etc. If expertise, money and support could be sustained in a network that retained these fluid mechanisms or value, then the system, its organisations, affiliates and individuals would become more resilient against outside force. Using alternative payment systems, social-media sites, means of communication, along with approaches such as crowd sourcing, personal favouritism and non-monetary barter/exchange/volunteering must be considered essential means of excluding outside interference, always with the knowledge that these means will be infiltrated and sabotaged.[11]

(K) The venue should be a centre of excellence and be designed, built, staffed and programmed to reflect the seriousness of dissident cultures, doing credit to dissident values by embodying them. Although established structures for long-standing art forms—the theatre, opera house, art gallery, seminar room, lecture auditorium—may allow traditional approaches to design and architecture, other elements—the cinema, car park, lifts, escalators, access ramps, vehicle access—may not

---

11   This is defined as "counter-economics" by the dissident left (Samuel Edward Konkin). "Per Bylund further organises the methodology of counter-economics into two strategies: the vertical and the horizontal. The vertical strategy involves dropping out of the structures of the State in order to rebuild the infrastructure and technology needed to support your chosen community at a smaller level. In real terms, this means creating networks of inter-reliance within the community without relying on outside structures or technology. [...] The horizontal strategy refers to the active participation and creation of black and grey markets—simply individuals truly voluntary trading with each other without State interference, proper free market and human action." Cameron P., "The Power of the Merchant", 7 December 2021, https://praxarchy.com/2021/12/07/the-power-of-the-merchant/, retrieved 7 March 2022

be amenable to traditional solutions or materials. This may involve making compromises in terms of architecture, especially when a degree of flexibility is needed. We should bear this in mind and exercise forebearance in terms of our personal tastes when decisions are made regarding design, not forgetting that reactionary politics does not perfectly equate to artistic conservatism.

IV

An Eisteddfod is an annual arts festival, primarily literary—comprising displays of recitation, poetry, singing and musical performance, art, craft and cultural accomplishment. A Welsh-nationalist revival (or recreation) of bardic gatherings, Eisteddfodau are both local and national in Wales, the Welsh diaspora and Celtic regions. In Wales, there are some that have participants who are local, national or international. The fact that most or all of Eisteddfodau are conducted in Welsh is a naturally limiting factor.

Welsh is a minority indigenous language even within Wales and is not spoken by any significant community outside of Wales today. The fact that almost 100% of all people who speak Welsh (as opposed to those instructed in at school and who recognise a few Welsh words) are indigenous Welsh or grew up in Wales is a problem for the progressive elite in Cardiff. The Welsh Arts Council commissioned a report in order to condemn its own national language as "racist and exclusionary".[12] This was entirely as they expected and intended. This indicates the level of disgust that the British governing elite has towards its indigenous population, which is as unsustainable as it is reprehensible, and a sure sign of impending collapse. No society headed by an elite that loathes its majority population can

12   https://www.independentsentinel.com/woke-wales-says-the-word-welsh-and-the-language-is-racist/, retrieved 16 October 2021.

long maintain its viability. This indicates the necessity of building an alternative network, ready to work for a new elite in an alliance with the population, not against it.

Now that state (and, increasingly, local) venues are programmed along quota lines, with demographic characteristics of creators' priorities over merit, ambitious and talented artists find themselves marginalised as never before. Traditionalists, and even apolitical artists, need to form their own networks. Any events need to eschew "diversity, inclusion and equity" (as conflicting with participant merits)—which will, *de facto*, render the events ineligible for state funding. Any attachment to criteria of excellence leads to demographically inequitable results and must therefore be not only avoided, but discredited, by a progressivist art elite adhering to leftist identity politics.

One route to displays of excellence could be an Eisteddfod organised by traditionalists and dissidents, one for the whole of the United Kingdom. (Additional local ones would also be beneficial.) A multi-arts festival held annually, in a different location each time (or on a rotating roster of locations) open only to British nationals or those born in Britain could be a way of encouraging creators locked out of a state-funded arts system which is hostile to them. However, if there is an established arts venue—the posited "based Barbican"—that could be a suitable site for a national Eisteddfod.

The content of the arts could be apolitical. In fact, I suggest that there be no political criteria for selection. The only bars should be entrants being British nationals and merit within the given field. Entrants should be judged anonymously, as far as possible. Prizes could be given; grants and scholarships could be awarded to promising practitioners aged under 25. Children's-level events should be arranged. Events would sell exhibited material, with the organisers taking a percentage to help fund the event.

Distinguished practitioners could be honoured with special displays or performances. Authors could be invited to read their works. Book signings would encourage sales and give authors income. Recitations from memory should be encouraged. Discussion panels and lectures could also take place in tandem. Livestreaming of performances, discussions and interviews could take place. For a voluntary fee, a commemorative book could be published and posted to ticket buyers after the event, including artwork, photographs and delivered texts from the event.

If the dissident arts centre had a publishing arm, then a high-quality annual book could be produced, offered generally. The centre might be able to hold a collection of Eisteddfod material, including scripts, photographs, interviews, prizewinning crafts and donated art works—which could be used in the centre—and books, which could become part of a specialist library-archive. The arts centre could become a cultural repository, accumulating a permanent collection.

These aims sound prosaically basic, almost quaint. An event that mixes high culture, crafts, trade, amateur performances and professional events seems so old fashioned that it is alien for generations raised on globetrotting star performers, foreign curators, international press junkets and cultural nabobs from the capital, all underwritten by public money. That is exactly why an Eisteddfod provides a refreshingly rooted alternative and why it is important to undertake. Contemporary high culture is deracinated because it lacks connection to local people and location—it is a moveable feast, put on by "anywhere" people for themselves—with events hardly able to be differentiated from a comparable event held in Geneva, Hong Kong, Barcelona or Miami. Globalist events command little local support or engagement because it is the culture of the elite, displayed to accentuate the distance between the elite caste and the general public which funds these events but is conspicuously alienated by them.

Such a scheme is ambitious at a national level, but we know these schemes can work. The key is to build incrementally, each year, consolidating gains and learning from mistakes. One thing we know is that such a project will face unremitting scorn, hostility and even disruption from the state, mass media and activist minions of the outer party. For doing what was normal in our lifetimes—setting up something little more than a county fair, with an emphasis of the arts—the participants will be pilloried as racists and xenophobes. But, in a world where simply speaking the truth and holding to one's beliefs is cast as being adjacent to moral atrocities, there is nothing honest we can do that will not be relentlessly assaulted by *globo homo*.

V

Any dissident arts centre will attract the ire of the governing elite. The mass media, pressure groups, politicians, rival arts venues and the majority of the governing and non-governing elite will actively oppose the venue. Everything from media hit pieces and petitions to zoning-regulation alterations and deplatforming from banking systems should be expected. Although, at that extreme level of the exertion of elite force, all dissident activity becomes narrowed to mere survival and the direct actions required for that purpose, with all cultural activity suspended. However, short of that point, it is worth pursuing the founding of an arts centre because it would offer a home and hub to alternative creators and allow genuinely skilled creators, curators and administrators to work without conforming to the political shibboleths of the current elite.

An arts centre should not be the only project, or even the main project, of dissidents in the cultural sector—that should be the establishment of a resilient network and a semi-independent economy—but it is a worthwhile project. It would function as a showcase for the values of those opposed to the liberalist/progressivist regime, whilst also nurturing talent based on merit, not demographic favouritism, and providing high-quality apolitical arts to the local population and visitors. If such a venue were to work organisationally, financially and artistically, it might provide evidence of viability of the core reactionary ideas for society as a whole, acting as an exemplar of dissenting principles put into practice. That, of course, is precisely why the liberalist/progressivist state will attempt to destroy it.

The potential is huge. Our ambitions need to be commensurately huge but grounded in reality; our assessment must be likewise realistic about the assaults such a project would face from the current governing elite. It is only one part of the challenge of making an alternative network of art, artists, collectors and art lovers who believe in true diversity—of styles, schools, materials, ideas—and are not blighted by progressivist criteria. The commercial-art sector offers a template, as does Stuckist activity. In some ways it is a daunting challenge, but the most daunting part is accepting that—as a dissident or simply not being a member of the state's client classes—your art will never gain admittance to the halls of State Art. Once you come to realise what has been the truth for five or ten years already, the future looks open rather than barren. Act as if State Art museums do not exist because—for you and me—they do not.

The establishment has turned its back upon you; it is time to turn your back on it. Start building for your future.

February-March 2022

FIVE

THE COVENTRY SPEECH

The reactionary creator, the progressive analyser

A capable artisan or scholar cuts a good figure if he have his pride in his art, and looks pleasantly and contentedly upon life. On the other hand, there is no sight more wretched than that of a cobbler or a schoolmaster who, with the air of a martyr, gives one to understand that he was really born for something better. There is nothing better than what is good![1]

So wrote Friedrich Nietzsche (1844-1900).

Devotion to making well is analogous to living out one's potential and this, according to Nietzsche, gives man's life meaning. For Nietzsche, alarmed at the in-roads made by rationalism and Enlightenment into the soul of man, the artist becomes a paradigm of man liberated from humanism, scientism, socialism and Christianity, who can go on to re-establish the foundational values of society. Here is Martin Heidegger on Nietzsche:

Art, thought in the broadest sense as the creative, constitutes the basic character of beings. Accordingly, art in the narrower sense is that activity in which creation emerges

1   Friedrich Nietzsche, Oscar Levy (trans.), *The Will to Power*, 1901, Foulis, London, 1933, pp. 64-5

36

> for itself and becomes most perspicuous; it is not merely one configuration of will to power among others but the supreme configuration. Will to power becomes genuinely visible in terms of art and as art. But will to power is the ground upon which all valuation in future will stand. It is the principle of the new valuation, as opposed to the prior one which was dominated by religion, morality, and philosophy. If will to power therefore finds its supreme configuration in art, the positing of the new relation of will to power must proceed from art.[2]

Will to power is the concept to consciously determine (or adopt) one's personal values and to impose those on the world around.

Nietzsche wrote that, "Art is the distinctive counter-movement to nihilism."[3] As art springs from conscious values, aesthetics is a field of meaning and social values expressed through culture. Art is creative—the assertion of values; nihilism is destructive—the negation of values. Nihilism is a rejection of the potential of contribution. It asserts a severance from the culture that came before and significance accorded to art. Nietzsche thought that a unified man—who combined the Dionysian passion and deep instinct with Apollonian order and rationality—was a reflection of a society that combined the halves of man's nature in a fruitful and honest manner. The artist was the exemplar of this.

The reactionary man is the Aristotelean man who embodies virtue rather than signalling it. He is driven by the impetus to create not to theorise. Theorisation can be the respectable counterpart of prevarication. The progressive man is sceptical, analytical; he appropriates and adapts. Whenever he cannot win his case through persuasion, he

2   Martin Heidegger, David Farrell Krell (trans.), *Nietzsche: Volume I*, 1961, Routledge & Kegan, 1981, p. 72

3   Nietzsche, quoted in Heidegger, 1981, p. 73

will manipulate and make changes secretly. Whatever a reactionary's ethics and aims are (generally speaking) they arise through acculturation and instinct—albeit a cultivated instinct or an inculcated instinct—not through theory. I am not speaking of strategy, tactics or politics here, but of an understanding of the world and of human nature. What the reactionary knows is from inherited wisdom or direct observation; it is not a fresh proposition, *ex nihilo*. The reactionary man can think but he sets no store on originality nor opening new fields of knowledge. Perhaps it is understandable that (given my circumstances) I reach for the artist as the template for reactionary anti-modern man.

Progressive man relies on the feminisation of public spaces, such as the museum, the library, the debating chamber, the university and the parliament, those institutions that reactionary man founded. Progressive man is feminised man. He has his uses, as long as is kept in his place, because we benefit from having men and women, weak and strong, passive and active, thinkers and doers, scientists and soldiers, priests and—dare I say?—merchants. Balance benefits us but only if the parts are kept in the correct proportion, which does not mean kept equal. Harmony comes through correct balance and knowing—intuiting even—the correct proportions and places for components. As with architecture and art, so with society.

Ugliness as a weapon against men

Here is Nietzsche on the impact of ugliness.

> Nothing is beautiful, except man alone: all aesthetics rests upon this naïveté, which is its *first* truth. Let us immediately add the second: nothing is ugly except the degenerating man—and with this the realm of aesthetic judgement is circumscribed. Physiologically, everything ugly weakens and saddens man. It reminds him of decay, danger, impotence; it actually deprives him of strength. One can

measure the effect of the ugly with a dynamometer. Whenever man is depressed at all, he senses the proximity of something 'ugly.' His feeling of power, his will to power, his courage, his pride—all fall with the ugly and rise with the beautiful.[4]

That man is the measure of all things is a common staple, dating back to the Roman Vitruvius and earlier. The earliest of philosophers of aesthetics knew that we reach for beauty aside from any consideration of material advancement. Making art was seen as a form of worship. The work of the *artista* (in ancient times the *artista* was any skilled fabricator of objects and even ideas) was a reflection of God as creator. The use of the objects and the stories people told about them afterwards—in connection to the maker, the original owner, other objects—became culture.

We recognise within ourselves a yearning for beauty and we feel an impact from the deprivation of beauty and the impact of ugliness. So much of our world is made ugly by new things. Buildings that are ugly and proportioned to intimidate turn our cities in places that bombards with impressions our weakness and insignificance. Even the fact that we cannot reject the forms of these buildings or tear them down—and the fact they are erected against our will, so often irrevocably altering a beloved skyline—is a power play, one designed to impress upon us our inferior status. That is, not just our current lowly position in a social hierarchy, but our status as a fallen society. It is no wonder that this leads us to revolt against the modern.

Old buildings of beauty are made ugly by the addition of new extensions that are crude and which seem designed to humiliate the building. It is a form of ritual shaming.

4   Nietzsche, *Twilight of the Idols*, 1889, quoted in Charles Harrison, Paul Wood, Jason Gaiger (eds.), *Art in Theory, 1815-1900*, Blackwell, Oxford, 2001, p. 786

Likewise, the noble forms of men and women are made ugly with tattoos and piercings. Modern persons makes themselves look ugly then dare you to be revolted, they make themselves absurd then dare you to laugh. They dare you to be judgemental then take offence at your response. Aposematism is when an animal develops protective coloration. A frog that is bright red and a snake that is yellow and orange are telling predators that they are poisonous and to keep away. When a person makes themselves look ugly, they are telling you that they feel ugly about themselves and that you should beware.

The environment of the city is being depleted of its historical character and turned into a node of international architecture. This is a deliberate campaign to demoralise us and displace historical associations, so that we become detached from place. It feeds into the progressive desire to rewrite history and rewrite people. This campaign says here is the new normal and you will never have the spiritual oneness that your forebears had. When we think of reactionary narratives, we think of words, of stories and values. Perhaps we should think in terms of places and objects. We can reject what we find offensive and hurtful—because it seems intended to hurt and demean us—and to build places with dignity and grace. There does seem this reluctance to commit to physical culture in our spheres. Much of that is to do with lack of funding, opportunity and permission but it does also seem an innate fear of failing. There seems a lingering reticence. Just as the online edgelord calls action in the real world "cringe", so even rich men are afraid of being mocked for their taste, if they were to commit to a building or painting, and being derided by the tastemakers of their time or even by their acquaintances. I cannot remember who made that observation, but there is a deep fear of being shamed by one's peers, most particularly in terms of cultural taste.

I would like to pay tribute here to those of us who have had the courage to risk failure and who have conspicuously committed with their money and reputations with events and actions in the non-online world. I am thinking here of Evelyn [Duncan] and John [Sweeney], Carl Benjamin and the Lotus Eaters, the Bournbrook Press team and not least the Scyldings Events organisers. They have all been brave enough to make a difference. If you wish to do the necessary work and want a share of the rewards, join us in making your commitment concrete now.

Logos and praxis

Tradition arises through the emergence of metaphysical truths that manifest themselves in custom, habit, repetition and the work of men (individually and collectively). The ideological and theoretical models of the world derived in isolation from observation of perennial truths must be progressive because they seek to usurp the natural order. Rather than assessing what is true and seeking to understand the tragic constrained vision of human nature (as the reactionary does), the progressive presupposes what ought to be then seeks to implement that utopian unconstrained vision, regardless of the truth of the world. This acceptance of our tragic limitations does not forestall acknowledgement that we are capable of great collective work but that such work only comes about if we know our human flaws, something the progressive utopian rejects.

Every society has stories it tells itself, that incorporates its values and nominates heroes and villains. Perhaps the way for us to write our story is by doing and allowing the story to emerge from our actions, from our physical culture, here and now. We should not theorise now but allow our narrative to rise out of what me make and what we choose to discard.

The theme of this conference is logos and praxis, from

a dissident perspective. Let's look at the dictionary definitions of "praxis": (1) exercise or practice of a skill; (2) the implementation of a concept in practice; (3) the testing of a theory through practice; (4) the realisation of ideas through application. Progressivism and liberalism are theory led and demand praxis. After all, as so many Neo-Marxists will tell you, there is no point in theory which does not result in action. It seems that to me there may be no praxis for a reactionary, only doing. For the religious among us, the issue is not praxis but duty—duty to our families, God, the wider clan and tradition. That entails no innovation only obedience and it requires leadership.

The reactionary sees himself as a spiritual being acting as an imperfect heir, one who seeks acceptance amongst his ancestors; the progressive sees himself as a material entity acting towards the betterment of humanity, of which he is the current culmination. For the reactionary, action is the following of deep tradition and enactment of natural law; in other words, there is no reactionary praxis.

The reactionary creator follows his instinct, hardly different to those of a huntsman. When he works, he gains an intuitive understanding of his tools and his materials. He know how the blade will twist in his hand, he can feel the grain of wood in the log, he knows the ring of true stone and clank of flawed stone when he raps it. I know how the paint will lie as I apply it and I could only know that through intuiting, with intuition the result of experience. This is the emergence of hidden truths that are uncovered by tutorship, experience, observation. This is internalised as a kind of muscle memory, which links him with his ancestors, a profound instinct that has a poetry to which men respond. This is akin to how the hunter knows the way an animal runs or how the matador knows where to place the sword. The progressive sees the bullfight as no sport at all and cheers the bull on, regardless of the qualities of the bull and the man, revealing an innate misanthropy. The reactionary knows the bullfight is no sport but sacrifice and a chance for man and beast to prove their valour. The bull's death is certain before he enters the arena, all that is to be decided is his quality before he dies.

The reactionary understands the truth due to doing. The progressive fails to understand due to thinking.

Interlude

I once gave a lecture at a university, in Aberystwyth, I think. There was an exhibition of my art there and I gave an illustrated talk about my career. At the end, there was a question-and-answer session. One of the art students asked "Should I become a full-time art?" I said,

> No. You've already answered your question. If you were suitable to be an artist, you would be asking me, how do I become an artist? How do I survive as an artist? I didn't have a choice. Art chose me. I knew I needed to make art; I just didn't know exactly how I could arrange my life around that activity. If you've got any doubt at all, then it isn't the right life for you. All the best art was made by people who were obsessed by art—by looking at it, by making it, sometimes (more rarely) by talking to others about it. Great art was never made by a dabbler, a talented amateur or someone who walked away from art. A great artist is obsessed. He feels he can always do better, not just better than himself but better than the greatest artists who ever lived.

Or that was roughly what I said. I remember he looked a bit crushed and I did feel a touch sorry for him. He was probably fishing for some pithy tip on how to get by as an artist and instead I ran my bulldozer over his dreams and crushed him flat. I now extend my apologies to him across the ether of indeterminate time and space. But I was right and I am sure he never became an artist.

How to Start a Dissident Art Movement

Male creators, female curators

Once an art work is made it goes off to live (and die) in the wider world, as part of the collections of private persons and companies and (less often) museums. We have entered a time when the paradigm is male creator, female curator. In the past, it would have been male creator, male curator, male collector but female buyer, for the woman (historically) makes the home and often decides the décor. With the entrance of women into the workplace, we see the museum become feminised. But [female curators] are not (as their male predecessors were) impelled by a duty to preserve and record, but to change. They introduce the concept of social justice into museums, which necessitates ritually shaming art works and seeking to remove art works. The process of deaccessioning—which is the technical term for museums permanently removing objects from their collections—is being pressed for by today's curators so that they may salve the historical wounds of underrepresentation of demographic groups. The women and over-socialised men who run our museums, and have not even the passing familiarity of the effort and skill it takes to make art, are on a crusade to reduce, to erase, to improve.

All of this is headed by the Museums Association, an organisation (established in 1889) dedicated to providing ethical guidance to museum staff. This is an association now run entirely by women and feminised men. Go to their website and among the promotional photographs you will barely find a male (or white) face. This is deliberate (as I found too for the National Trust, as described in my book *Artivism*). These are the managerial non-governing class hard at work under the hood, reorganising the engine of culture. They have never built an engine, they have never serviced one competently, they do not understand the principles but they are sure they can alter an engine to be more equitable. Of course, it is inequality, hierarchy, exceptionality, cussed unbowed individuals selected by the grace of God or the shuffling of their genes to be geniuses who are the engine of culture. The Pareto Principle tells us it is those exceptional individuals who do the meaningful work. Once you start to change that engine—or build it from scratch—selecting the engine parts on the basis of their shininess or feeling sad about those parts that historically get excluded from engines, you've broken your engine and broken your vehicle and I suppose, as you sit there sulking, you can claim you only had good intentions.

Except that you never did have good intentions. You improvers, you tweakers, you meddlers, you women, you were always driven by resentment—a topic Nietzsche covered at length. Egalitarianism is not kindness; it is resentment at the unbending unfairness of the world, at the imperious inflexibility of nature, at the power of the divine. Egalitarianism is a revolt against God, Nature and proper order, that reveals itself to the contemplator and seeker of truth. A craftsman will tell you that types of woods are not made equal and that the blunt blade is not only a danger to the wielder, it is an insult to the wood, it is slander to the tradition. The worker knows there has never been equality between men, between men and women, between animals and men, between any things in the world. He knows it because he lives it. He knows what ropes will support which weight. The maker, the doer, the reactionary man who understands the world through action learns the truth and knows that a lie will ruin the stone, break the tool, topple the structure, kill the man.

That is why I say to you, as an artist, beware the woman or the progressive man given any power to control a machine he or she did not build, to run any organisation they did not found, to command any society at all.

As we speak, the doors the museums' store rooms are open and women and over-socialised men are filling the stores with the art of women, ethnic and sexual minorities and foreigners who are chosen precisely for such reductive reasons, because they are who they are. And this is done because those curators of today cannot help being who they are. They are contaminating our patrimony with mediocrity. They are farmers who shovel in grit into a silo of wheat because they feel sorry for the grit. They are the drivers of a car with an internal-combustion engine who fill their fuel tank with water, because water in the most plentiful liquid on the planet and surely it is time water gets its chance to show what it can do. And believe me, water will get its chance.

We must be mad to have let this happen. What comes to mind is Shakespeare's *Othello* and the line, "Oh God, that men should put an enemy in their mouths to steal away their brains!" Except, of course, they did not do that to themselves. It was done to them.

Salvador Dalí

What would keep a reactionary artist going? Praise, exposure, companionship (if he is that way inclined), enough money to keep a roof over his head. But there comes a time when he must choose between art and a family. In some cases it is literally to decide between making art alone or marrying and giving up art. The lucky ones find a way to combine family with making art, but too often the world is deprived of either the art or the children and if the reactionary man is worth anything as an artist or as a man then it is a loss to us overall. In the Renaissance, art would be a family affair. The father would be the master in the studio, the wife would handle the money and tradesmen, the children would model or work as assistants. The idea of a whole family—even an extended family—living off the income of one earner is quite distant from us.

Here are two reflections on one dissident artist. This

came up as part of research for my next book (*Dalí*, Prestel, 2023) and future writings on reactionary aesthetics.

When the filmmaker Luis Buñuel (1900-1983) wrote to his friend Salvador Dalí (1904-1989) in 1939, he was asking for a loan. The pair had met as students in Madrid and had gone on to make two masterpieces of transgressive cinema *Un Chien andalou* (1929) and *L'Age d'or* (1930). At that time both of them (as Surrealists) had publicly supported Communism and anti-clericalism and did so throughout the 1930s. Dalí was threatened with expulsion from the French Surrealist group by leader in 1934. Breton accused him of "counter-revolutionary acts tending to the glorification of Hitlerian Fascism".[5] The expulsion was only rescinded after Dalí signed a document declaring himself to be an ally of the proletariat.

By the time of Buñuel's letter—1939—things had changed. Franco had won the Spanish Civil War; Dalí had moved from being at the darling of the Surrealist movement to being on its fringes; Dalí was also a very rich man by this stage, which was (of course) why Buñuel was writing to him. Dalí was a celebrity and the wealthiest artist in America. Dalí became rich through selling art to Hollywood movie producers, New York socialites and French aristocrats. This gave the artist independence from the Surrealists and the largely politically left-wing and socially liberal milieu of his era. Dalí no longer had to make a pretence of solidarity with the proletariat or conforming to Communist ideology. Dalí would be the only Surrealist to express admiration for Hitler or Franco. At the end of Dalí's reply to Buñuel he decided that, on balance, he would not loan Buñuel any money. Buñuel was a supporter and advocate for left-wing causes antithetical to Dalí's values

5   Ian Gibson, *The Shameful Life of Salvador Dalí*, Faber & Faber, London, 1997, p. 393

and wellbeing.[6] Whatever one's personal aesthetic taste, it is undeniable that Dalí went on to paint (in the 1950s) some of the most significant religious paintings of the Twentieth Century. Had he remained tied—artistically, socially and financially—to the Surrealist group that was committed to Communism and anti-theism, he would not have created his religious works.

Dalí produced religious paintings expressing the wonder and power of the revealed wisdom of Catholic Christianity but he himself was not religious. He did not (as a rule) go to mass nor perform good works. He did not believe in the afterlife and his private life was far from pious. He was as materialistic as any non-Christian. Yet, his devotional painting is a brilliant *coup de theatre*, which advanced the case for mystical Christianity in an era (viewed at a continental level) that was hostile towards Christianity. So, clearly, you will now be thinking of Dalí as a propagator of Catholic mysticism in terms of a bifurcated logos and praxis. Or you could just call him a hypocrite. Yet Dalí did not believe in following the teaching of the Church but he believed in himself and his ability to make astonishing images that might strengthen the faith of Catholics and cement Franco's Spain as a place that upheld traditional values and produced new art.

Ultimately, although it is opportunity that allows artists to produce and express freely, the character within— the differences between reactionary man and progressive man—are matters of temperament and breeding. Dalí made a very bad Communist artist and much better Catholic artist and that was not decided by opportunity.

---

6   It should be noted that Dalí also had some personal scores to settle with his former collaborator, including being edited out of the credits of *L'Age d'or*. See Gibson, pp. 392-7

Action not praxis

To conclude, let us briefly go over the actions we can take to embody our values and transmit them to others. Rather than praxis, I suggest we revive and restore to use forms that existed before the era of tax-funded, state-directed culture. We must redouble our efforts to build strong networks of collaboration and patronage. Again, that involves working privately, establishing apprenticeships and stipends, arranging open and curated exhibitions, celebrating local talent, publishing new art, spurning the nodes of globalist culture, building our alternative economy.

I cannot speak about crypto-currency but I can reaffirm that using cash as often as possible is vital. It is the only guarantee of privacy and security. Just as Environmental and Social Governance exists to impose and increase globalism and progressivism through financial governance and corporate policy, so we must develop our own networks. These might be businesses we ourselves have a role in, family businesses or local firms—or even sympathetic overseas bodies. They might also be simply firms or individuals we know have not bought into [Environmental and Social Governance], progressivism and social justice.

Buy books and buy art. Buy physical copies of journals, consider contributing texts or donating to them. I have in mind *Bournbrook Magazine*, *The Jackdaw*, *The Mallard*, *The Salisbury Review*, the forthcoming journal *Advance*. A subscription or gift subscription is worthwhile, as many of these outlets teeter on the precipice of financial loss. Buy books from Imperium, Rogue Scholar, Imprint Academic and Bournbrook Press. Physical copies of media are as essential as using cash.

Finally, I recommend we resist and demonstrate our resistance. That means identifying and removing opponents through lawfare, public pressure and back-channel methods. This is suggested without illusions. When I helped to take down a political operative who was a director of the ICA gallery in London, I knew the replacement would be essentially the same. I knew the system would protect itself and that there would be no actual change.

I was the only critic in the middle of his career (rather than at the end) who was public in this action. Any critics or commentators who wish to be taken seriously by us—or want to receive any favourable treatment from us, should we be in a position to assist—must make themselves known now, at the crucial time, not wait until the balance has shifted in our favour. Show your courage and stand with me publicly. Soon enough, we shall be joined by others.

Systemic change is not possible due to replacement of individuals because the individual is not important. An individual is only appointed to such a position if they have negligible will and independence, only if they are totally subordinate to the elite. When we force them to show that purported accountability is fake, that regulations are not enforced, that the corruption in the system goes to the top and that no elected political party will be permitted to reform the system, we get them to expose themselves. This demonstrates to ourselves and to our sympathisers (and opponents) that we understand our situation, that we reject their values and we do not concede that they have a legitimate hold over anything they have not built. We signal to potential defectors and allies in the non-governing elite that we exist and that we will not back down because the beliefs of the elite are repugnant to us and we have superior values. We resist to show others and ourselves the we have the courage to defend our values, our patrimony and our people without apology and without quarter.

25 August 2022; delivered 28 August,
University of Warwick, Coventry.
Originally entitled
"Reactionary Praxis: Inventing Tradition".

HIGH RISK, HIGH REWARD:

THE REACTIONARY TEMPERAMENT IN THE ARTS

Under electric lights, seated men watch the dealer turn over playing cards on the green baize. Glasses of whisky and brandy are at their elbows, chips stacked high or low, a thin veil of cigar smoke just above bowed heads...

Last month I read stories by Knut Hamsun on men ruined by gambling. Hamsun was a big gambler, spending his royalties from his novels *Hunger*, *Mysteries* and *Pan* in Danish casinos. Despite his literary fame and financial success, Hamsun's gambling fever put his marriage at risk and threatened him with bankruptcy. This led me to an idea about risk, temperament, and vanguardism, specifically in relation to reactionary creators.

We should distinguish conservatives from reactionaries. Temperamentally, conservatives are aligned with liberals and socialists. They are risk averse. Conservatives value continuity, stability and predictability: anti-risk qualities. Together with socialists, they value conformity and group cohesion. They prioritize the socialization of risk and cost—conservatives through family and local community, socialists through the welfare state.

These people are far removed from the risk-taking, disagreeable, headstrong loners of the archetypes of the pioneer, explorer, prospector, athlete and warrior. In the early Twentieth Century, these kinds of men saw themselves as Nietzschean *Übermenschen*, who separated themselves from the received morality of the herd in a quest for truth. They visited unknown places and climbed unconquered peaks at great hazard to themselves, not knowing if what they attempted was even possible.

As the mechanical age of exploration arrived and the whole world was either colonized or organized into nation-states, these ventures came to an end—except in the arts, where there were still formal, material, conceptual, and moral barriers that could be overcome. It took promethean heroes to break free of salesrooms and academy ateliers in order to flatten the pictorial plane, abolish figuration, depict the unspeakable and advocate the unthinkable. If you failed, you would be classed insane or (even worse) unprofessional, dying impoverished and unknown. Yet the rewards were immense.

Consider Picasso. An academically proficient painter who became associated with mild modernism in Madrid and Barcelona, Picasso then moved to Paris, where intense personal rivalry with more ambitious vanguardists lead him to develop Cubism. His appetite supercharged the breaking of a path of innovation. Not for nothing did he compare himself and his colleague Georges Braque to two mountaineers, tied together while scaling an unclimbed summit. In his early years, he risked everything because he knew he could forge a path no other man could.

Picasso was a loyal member of the French Communist Party, but I cannot believe that either he or Ernest Hemingway—both of whom had seen death in the bullring—ever properly squared that raw reality with the political formulations of socialism and communism. Hemingway and Picasso shied away from the political implications of their insights into the tragic vision of man's nature.

The painter Francis Bacon was another example. Bacon was notoriously a big risk-taker, a heavy drinker and profligate with money. He was reckless in sex and his relationships cost him work. His lover Peter Lacy destroyed valuable Bacon paintings in alcohol-fuelled rages. Bacon was also a gambler, both winning and losing vast fortunes at the roulette wheel. After running underground gambling evenings in Blitz-era London—gambling on multiple levels, you might say—Bacon left for Monte Carlo to spend the late 1940s living from gambling rather than painting.

In his painting, Bacon often courted failure. He ruined great pictures by overworking them in search of a more intense, extraordinary outcome. He impetuously destroyed paintings he thought failures, only to later regret it. Bacon was gambling in the studio as much as he did in any casino.

Thomas Sowell has written of high rewards accrued by early adopters and vanguard figures and their unique psychological qualities. Pioneers of new movements are adventurous, independent, free-thinking, disagreeable and asocial. Most importantly, they are intense and committed. They stake everything. This is the epitome of the vanguardist as risk-taker, gambler, hunter, ground-breaker.

These loners are usually not collegial. They don't make good leaders because they don't obey rules. Then as soon as rewards are won by the small group of vanguardists, figures of lesser quality arrive in their wake: careerists and followers, exploiting opportunities rather than being committed to visions. They form a cadre of second-wave patrons, commentators, organizers, dealers, publishers, and critics, who disseminate the counter-elite's ideas and values of the new elite group.

What distinguishes the vanguard from the followers is risk-taking temperament and behaviour. Risk-takers are natural individualists. They understand the tragic vision of man bound to primitive drives which can never be overcome and which must be respected. Risk-takers are compelled to go into unmapped territory *because* it is unmapped.

José Ortega y Gasset's 1925 essay "The Dehumanization of Art" decried Modernist detachment from the values of the past. He was sanguine about elitism—art on a sociological level was, as Gasset noted, a means for a distinct class of individuals to recognise their shared minority status—but he regretted the revolt against reality and the narrowing of the scope of art. Modernism (Cubism, Futurism) went beyond Romanticism. "It is essentially unpopular; moreover, it is antipopular [...] It divides the public into two groups: one very small, formed by those who are favorably inclined towards it; another very large—the hostile majority." Acceleration towards territory so new and unfamiliar that it elicits not merely dislike but actual aggressive rejection might in part be due to risk-taking loners engaging in a competition to see who can take the most vanguard position.

The formal and conceptual extremism of the visual fine arts—caused by competition between risk-taking men, fuelled by the money of status-chasing patrons—have sped Western culture from Modernism to Post-Modernism in barely over a century. The same space of time has elapsed between Courbet's *Stonebreakers* (1850) and Walter de Maria's *Lightning Field* (1977) as between the birth of Leonardo da Vinci (1452) and the death of Titian (1576). This rapid sequence of art concepts and schools has provided us with richness but the drive for originality (or novelty, depending on your perspective) led to a greater distancing between the elite and the mass population, unwilling or unable to accept the parade of new concepts and styles.

A reactionary vanguard paints exciting pictures that show society the vital brutishness of life, reminding the comfortable of the animal within ourselves, but you wouldn't want them running your academies, teaching your children or managing your money. Conversely, conservatives might be the best custodians of tradition, but their art is often terribly dull. What is the solution?

Reactionaries will always be lumbered with risk-averse, social-conforming conservatives, and conservatives will always resent the unpredictable, perverse, untameable reactionary explorers. Ultimately, a territory cannot be won without risk-taking individuals, and a territory cannot be held without risk-averse individuals. We should just let each play their role and hope the gamble pays off.

February 2023

SEVEN

OUR NEXT STEPS: COMPONENTS OF AN ART MOVEMENT

Recently, a group of artists including me set up an exhibition in London. However, it is very unlikely that you will see museums acquire any of our art. Although some museums have art by me, that was before I distanced myself from contemporary fine art through my criticism of feminism, the women's art lobby, quota programming and eco-alarmism as a curatorial shibboleth.

What are the elements that comprise an art or cultural movement? Here are the components. They naturally develop sequentially.

Artists

The artists tend to come first. They do not come out of nowhere. They grow up in a culture and are trained by a system with which they have disagreements. They disagree with a culture in terms of the type of art that is appreciated, most particularly contemporary art; regarding the system, they reject the values, styles and techniques that are promoted or considered valid. As these artists grow apart from the majority of their peers, they grow closer to renegade figures and form brotherhoods or associations that better reflect their taste and ambitions. They share dreams and write manifestos; they paint and draw each other; they exhibit together. Their collectors come to know the art of other artists through introductions and encountering it through publications and displays.

The artists who gather together are likely to transmit their tastes and approach and to absorb the same from their colleagues. While this does not entail that the art produced will increasingly converge and form a singularity, it is true that the movement will produce art that has greater cross-influence than otherwise. Even though it may be limited to touches, colours, motifs and so forth, the art of this movement will become more linked and consistent rather than the reverse. It will become less atomised and more co-mingled. The more the ideas, values, subjects and materials are adjacent or overlapping, the more this process is accelerated.

Collectors and audience

When a new art emerges, it will appeal to an audience. That audience may wish to take up a new fashion or return to a dormant past tradition or they may wish to follow artists who are friends or characters that they admire. Some of those viewers will wish to own that art, either to support the artists (and their values) or to acquire art that they like. Some of them will wish their names to be known and associated with the movement. Another motivation is the desire to own artefacts that display their affinities, wealth and discrimination. These motivations are not detached from material considerations, such as these artefacts will increase in value. Trading in art increases. Completists want to own collections of all prints by an artist. Others want to acquire maquettes or small versions of acclaimed pieces by sculptors. Patrons commission portraits of spouses and family members by these artists.

Gallerists

When artists who have no strong ties to existing systems, such as academies (where they do not teach), open exhibitions (which will not exhibit their art) and galleries (which will not sell their art), there is obviously an opening for mediators. One mediator is the gallerist, who can take from the artist the burden of dealing with collectors and arranging viewings and deliveries. This is a commercial opportunity for a dealer, who acts as a bridge between artist and his established collectors. However, the increase profits and broaden the collector base for the artist—imagine what would happen if the artist (and later dealer) depended solely upon one collector, who might stop buying suddenly—the dealer has to expand the number of buyers. This does not have to be an indiscriminate popularisation. Art (at the top level) is a luxury good and its cachet in part depends on exclusivity, so a gallerist does not aim to reach as many buyers as possible, just the best buyers, and keep the price point high and restrict supply. So, do not equate the entrance of gallerists with a movement selling out. Some artists may give in to commercial temptations and dilute their originality, style and commitment to core values, but also consider the influence other way. Viewed in terms of elite theory, we are more likely to see the artists and their allies alter the market towards their values. Consider the way Surrealism was seen as grotesque and shocking, being mere nonsense of no artistic value. Surrealism was seen as nothing more than cartoon-strip japes transferred to the walls of the gullible. Now people may still disapprove of Surrealism, but it is taken more seriously, even if ultimately it is described as an aberration.

Critics

Part of the apparatus of a new movement is the appearance of critics, who take trouble to learn about the movement and explain its principles, personnel and values. They then discern between the levels of seriousness and accomplishment of the participants in the movement. They write reviews, profiles and conduct interviews. They are invited to write catalogue essays, then artist monographs or biographies. These critics are sometimes already established when the movement begins. Others are more closely bound to the movement and can be minor artists with a talent for writing (and suitable connections to get that writing read). These latter critics are more advocates than anything else and they see their success as tied to the prestige of the movement. They work naturally to make the movement more coherent, more vanguard, more important than perhaps it warrants, because the importance of the movement makes its arbiters-cum-experts commensurately more powerful.

Salons

The need to associate and co-ordinate leads to socialisation. In the past, cafés, bars and restaurants were meeting places for artists, models, critics and collectors; eventually, these places became so well known for this reason that fans travelled to hang out there and meet their heroes. To a degree we now have virtual salons—the Discord chat room and the chat function and comment section of the livestream. We recognise characters, public figures drop in, debates rage and jokes are made. However, the importance of meeting in real life is great. When we meet in life, forming human connections is easier and the consequential ties are deeper. The difficulty is that movements in the past were generally based on geography. The Schools of Barcelona, Delft, Paris, New York, London, St Ives and untold others consisted of artists who (for at least for a time) lived within walking distance of each other. Some semi-public spaces became venues where are art was exhibited or donated by the habitués. El Quatre Gats and La Lapin agile hosted what became the first public displays of this new art. Before the galleries of the Paris Right Bank or the museums of the New York Upper East Side were conquered, the coffee houses and cafeterias were decorated by the art of new movements.

Of course, members of a movement generally just prefer to go to certain establishments. They don't set up their own cafés specifically to serve them and their friends. Over time, these places may become reliant on such patronage but most establishments survive the demise of movements (and vice versa). They are not essential, because artists and their circles often meet in homes or attend public events together. There was the tradition of the literary salons held by hosts (or more often by hostesses), who would invite luminaries to converse; in this way hosts became acquaintances of artists and younger figures were introduced to the great creators. These were a development of the upper-class "at-home", when one set an afternoon once per week and opened one's sitting room to allow visitors to call in person. It is a shame that such personal contact is more difficult because of the geographical distribution of new art movements. For example, in our movement, artists live in the USA, Belgium, Montenegro and various parts of England. Despite putting on our show, we have never all met at the same time and some members have never met each other.

Publishing

Publication of catalogues, books, newsletters and manifestos accompany every art movement. Much of this is done via self-publishing because the established channels do not see the value of this material, that is when they do not actively disapprove of it. Self-publishing is now a lot easier due to print-on-demand services and online selling. Nonetheless, even today people who specialise in printing and selling this material are of great benefit to artists, who are not best suited for the manufacture and distribution of printed matter. There are many opportunities for publishing houses and distributors (in our case, primarily *IM-1776, Bournbrook Press, The Jackdaw* and *The Mallard*) for those who run a business of publishing. As our movement grows, so demand for written material and reproductions grow. There is no need for the artists themselves to do this work because it is best handled by others who can give it their expertise and time.

These are the initial stages for the first few years of a movement. The role of historians and museums is a matter for the later period, when these first stages are long established. These are stages that arise usually without explicit guidance from the artists involved. They come about because the logic of a movement and the economic and social imperatives that govern human interaction compel them. Watch for these stages, because these will soon arise with our own art movement. If they do not, there will be no movement because movement implies momentum and power. It is the power of money and prestige that will cause collectors to emerge, gallerists take on selling opportunities, critics to write and publishers to disseminate information.

We thrive or the movement dies. There is no halfway position.

31 July 2023

EIGHT

I'M NO OLD MASTER, NOR ARE YOU

When I was in my late teens and early twenties, I had an idea of my ideal home. It would be—if a country house with hillside views were not available—a place in Chester. The historic city of Chester, located on the English side of the England-Wales border, was founded by the Romans and primarily known for its historic half-timbered rows houses with arcades bounded by the (partially reconstructed) Roman city walls. Ever since the Victorian period, and the opening of a shopping arcade within the older buildings, Chester has been a destination town for the shoppers, holidaymakers and those attending the local racecourse. Chester is the epitome of (in the modern view) good urban design: compact, efficient, interlinked, pedestrianised—in addition to being very historic and very pretty. It was a city I knew well.

This choice accorded with what I wanted to do as an artist when I was young. When I arrived in London as an art student, I wanted to make art that engaged with the Old Masters, using the same materials and motifs but (in a Modernist rather than Post-Modernist manner) using the fragment aesthetic to mark out my distance from that lineage, as well as my admiration. I wanted to be the latest (or, if I admit my ego fully, the last) Old Master. I made drawings of figures in dark rooms, in Rembrandtian mode; I etched a Bellini throne in a hollow interior, scratchy and rough; I transcribed Titian's *Assumption of the Virgin*. I saw myself graduating from college in London and returning to live in Chester, making art in the old style, surrounded by buildings that (if you half-closed your eyes) might be taken for a street unchanged from the Sixteenth Century. As a 20-year-old student artist I had an Old Master complex.

Then I began to have doubts. It was not that I did not think myself incapable of reaching the technical standards and experience-based judgement necessary; I changed course, so no accurate assessment could be made about my potential as a follower of the Old Masters. It was not a case of me embracing Post-Modernism or the social activism of humanitarian egalitarianism or spurning the elitism of past art. It was that I became aware that my position was self-conscious. I was thinking about myself as an artist rather than thinking solely about the art, and real art comes about when one abandons the self and submits oneself to the imperatives of the picture and conveying meanings or values. One literally loses oneself as one follows intuition. The art that I made when I was most passionate and engaged was not traditional in form. I could not honestly paint like an Old Master because what I was responding to—albeit often in a negative way—was what around me: photographs, abstract art, Conceptualism, film, music. Maybe there is a way to draw like Raphael while listening to Post-Rock or thinking about newspaper photographs (I can think of a few artists today in that field) but it was not for me. Thinking of myself not just as the latest Old Master but just as an artist at all, was not so much inhibiting me as disabling me.

This lesson was reinforced when I made paintings of trees. There are no pure landscapes in classical art, although classical art includes landscape, and there is little that could be described as landscape art before Pieter Bruegel the Elder. So, painting trees and documenting land purely had no exact precedent from the Renaissance to follow. Thus freed, I committed myself to the truth of the source and the necessities of the pictures, setting aside artistic precedents.

Thinking of oneself as an artist while making art is death for art. It initiates the invidious process of being directed by expectations of what people will think of my art, how I should be as an artist, what sort of material I should be making. It is, effectively, looking over one's shoulder, inviting compliments and exclamations. It kills vigorous art in its tracks. To make great art, the artist must abandon all expectations and thought of an audience and submit oneself entirely to making the art, doing what needs to be done, however counter-intuitive or unprecedented. And some of that art will fail. Art benefits from its maker being free in the studio and cautiously critical once out of the studio, when it comes time to exhibit, publish and sell that art. Of course, that does not endorse self-indulgence or the fallacy of art at its apex being an uncriticisable expression of self. Artists must be disciplined but not self-conscious, free but not slapdash, inventive but not rambling. It is a difficult balance and if someone reading this description were to feel exasperated by such a fine subjective line being advocated, I would entirely sympathise. We should remember that great artists are truly exceptional and they can perform such delicate balances intuitively, making fine negotiations without being consciously aware of it.

I realised that living in a city such as Chester would immerse me in a world where I could tell myself comforting lies about being a living Old Master. It would actively damage both the art I made and the way I conducted myself. So I gave up that aspiration with as little sense of loss, as if I were renouncing a plan to build a time machine or [relinquishing my destiny to become] the ruler of the world.

What about the Pre-Raphaelites and those other artists who looked to the past? The Pre-Raphaelites, the Nazarenes, the Arts & Crafts groups and other historicist movements made art that was self-consciously retrograde. Yet what one finds with each is that they reflect the taste, aptitude and limitations of their era more explicitly and deeply than they realised. There is no danger of even a moderately educated layman mistaking a John Everett Millais for a Perugino or a Gabriel Dante Rossetti for a Veronese. They made art that comes from their own time. For the harshest critics (including conservative ones), the historicists are engaging in theatre, deluding themselves. Following such revivalist movements leads to what we have found in the chain of adoption-quotation in commercial graphic art inspiring Pop Art inspiring Post-Modernist art, with each stage of digestion extracting less nutritional content. Without going to some new raw source of content, artists risk quoting each other in ever-diminishing circles, each becoming a weaker imitation of the last iteration, meaningful content dwindling inexorably.

Artists in a living tradition produce art that addresses subjects and expresses values that need to be transmitted, using new forms and materials when available. Aside from narrative/value content and aesthetic qualities, they do not neglect the documentational function of art. Art can record our lives in a relatively neutral way (admitting that any selection implies viewpoint) but can add layers of criticism or celebration. Even if we find ourselves condemning the art produced, that art survives to tell us how it was to live at that time—be that the glorious heights of the Assyria Empire in Nimrud and the Parthenon of Phidias or the depths of Weimar desperation and depleted materialistic of 1990s Britain, as found in BritArt.

So often we see in reactionary and dissident circles

scorn regarding non-traditional art. In some respects, this is understandable as those non-traditional forms have been linked to propositions of liberalist values. I fully understand these suspicions, having studied and written about this subject for 30 years. To supporters of traditional art being made today I would say, yes, by all means support the art that you enjoy and care about but do not go out of your way to attack art made by artists who are politically sympathetic but who work in non-traditional ways. If you want a living movement that generates art of seriousness and power, that art will not be one that wholly replicates techniques and subjects of the Old Masters.

In their times, Giotto, Donatello, Raphael, Titian and Rembrandt were revolutionary artists who broke many conventions—that caused them to be esteemed and condemned in their own times. When vital art is made, it must include some new material or realities of its age, as it did in the age of Old Masters. Titian painted in ways that were considered unorthodox—painting without fixed compositional designs, not using underdrawing, leaving visible rough brushwork, neglecting "finish". Rembrandt depicted light as much as describing material, using broad style and ordinary implements in addition to paintbrushes. Watteau made cool social commentary by having his upper-class subjects dressed in contemporary *commedia dell'arte* costumes, using a new *trois crayons* technique for his drawings. (My thoughts on Vermeer's innovations will be found in next year's book, published by Prestel.) For each significant artist (from the ancient Greeks up to today), we could point to innovation in themes, motifs, materials and techniques. If you want new Titians and Rembrandts, you will have to accept that they will be awkward customers, cussed and shocking. The art that they produce may be ugly and awkward as often as it is beautiful. After all, the truths it will assert are difficult to acknowledge as they remind us of our fallibilities.

In short, if you are thinking of yourself as the latest Old Master, then you cannot be one. If the Old Masters came about through innovation, to add to their lineage you too must be an innovator and you must be of your time. I do not say you should be an abstract painter or Conceptualist, but I do say your art will not like something made in a previous century. If you want to be a stonemason diligently following the line of your forebears then I am glad for you, but you will be an artisan (a noble enough role!) not an Old Master. An Old Master (of any era) has never been, at heart, a follower or an imitator. The title of Old Master is bestowed posthumously by others, not appropriated by the artist himself.

Although most artists today who are avowed tradition-alists fight shy of describing themselves as Old Masters, it is apparent that they see themselves as in a direct line from them. Too often the Old-Master mentality in artists today is a way of sidestepping the real challenge—making vitalist art that upholds eternal values but reflects something of today. To traditionalist artists, I say that I respect your dedication and ability and I love your heroes no less than you do, but I fear that if you want to preserve and renew traditionalist values and to save art, you are going about it the wrong way. I support your right to make the art you choose. I refrain from criticising you as individuals because I feel kinship with you and admire your abilities. I was one of you. Consider my points. Join me, if you feel you can.

26 August 2023

NINE

BAD PAINTING, FOLK ART AND LOCALISM

Say you want to counter a trend which is reducing fine art to a cycle of cautious, state-approved bromides that defang art and undermine national identity. What happens if that opposition works...but you end up with art that might be just as bad?

If we define ourselves in negatives, by identifying what we reject—as so many emerging groups or movements do—we will likely find ourselves in uncharted territory. For example, let us say that we oppose the globalised art market as a framework for producing new art. Globalist art's expansion and hegemony—as measured at the highest strata of publishing, selling, exhibiting, museum acquisitions and auction prices—is antithetical to the development of art that answers to the axiomatic principles of truth, beauty and joy, and which is non-egalitarian and non-utilitarian in character. The opposite of globalist art is localist art. That is what I have previously advanced as an alternative to state-directed state-serving art. After all, in the absence of a realistic prospect of securing control of central power, one must oppose it and find routes to cultivate new art of value. The best way to oppose centralised dissemination of cultural material intended to undermine national customs is to encourage a decentralised localism that can sustain itself without central control. And the outcome of that localism would be.... well, what exactly?

The case of localists is that if the malefic globalist avant-garde has its grip on the consciousness of the country loosened, a population of artists—once free of top-down direction—will naturally gather into nodes of regional, national or ethnic identity. The pull of authentic subjects will draw artists together in common cause. Yet, is that really what would happen? In a society so deracinated—that is, literally, "unrooted"—is there any *Volksgefühl* still extant which could manifest?

There are no shortage of artists and commentators agitating for regional and national schools of art that might provide an alternative to the art of Jeff Koons, Damien Hirst, Richard Prince, Anthony Gormley, Yue Minjun, Yayoi Kusama and other brands one finds cluttering up the museum and art-fair schedules worldwide. As debates rumble on about exactly how the shoddiness of the modern world is to be confronted and remediated in all areas of culture, we have seen a resurgence of support for traditional painting. This tradition is of a limited kind and centres upon the art of French Naturalists, academic German Romantics, Victorian salon painters, Impressionists, Art Nouveau and fantasy artists. Common subjects are women in meadows, children in traditional dress, heroic men, pristine wildernesses, wild animals and so forth.

The art these objectors make or recommend looks conventional and laboured. Would galleries full of new art of this type inspire in a discerning visitor anything other than disappointment? Wouldn't a viewer want something more ambitious and (not in a modish way) of his own time rather than strategically timeless? I have already expressed my doubts about this.[1]

---

1   See "I'm No Old Master, nor are You"

Let us say a genuinely decentralised culture emerged and was allowed to flourish. What sort of art would arise among the next generation, freed from the grip of liberalism and Post-Modernism? What would the blossoming of a new Folk Art—made by local people, arising from local needs, embedded in the lives of people detached from metropolitan mores and civil-service diversity quotas—look like? The answer may not appeal to you.

Recently I visited H MKA, the Antwerp museum of contemporary art, where I saw Jim Shaw's current exhibition *The Ties That Bind*.[2] That includes his collection of amateur paintings bought at flea markets and junk shops. These Thrift Store Paintings have been exhibited widely and published, usually without data on the artist, title or origin of individual pictures. The art is a mixture of portraits, fantasy, erotica, pin-ups, decorative abstraction, Americana. Terrible Surrealism, rip-offs, faux naïf and appalling montages dominate. Anatomy is wayward, faces asymmetrical, poses stilted, landscapes garish, colours clashing. In cheap frames, crudely painted and ghastly in every way, they form a riot of bad taste. Hung edge to edge, the paintings are intended to be a spectacle, an experience, rather than seen in isolation.

The Thrift Store Paintings have a raw energy and genuine engagement that we cannot find in the high art exhibited at prestige venues. At the same time, consuming low art in any quantity—unavoidably so, in the H MKA display—leaves one with a sense of emptiness. It is like eating too much confectionary. It has little nutritional value, leaves you unfulfilled and will give you a headache; in the long run, it will numb you and make you ill. Yet it has the spark of real enthusiasm, not tempered by the expectations

2   "Jim Shaw: The Ties that Bind", *H MKA*, 16 February-19 May 2024

of audience, market and history.

The Thrift Store Paintings are gruesomely funny; we are supposed to laugh, which (if we know anything about taste and culture) we do. Yet, the Thrift Store Paintings are actual living Folk Art. Staring dazedly at the freak show of bad art surrounding me, it occurred to me that the future of art in a post-Internet, decentralised, populist universe would look a lot more like the Thrift Store Paintings than any 21ˢᵗ century Pre-Raphaelite Brotherhood. Rather than a nativist culture that most perennial traditionalists and reactionaries expect would grow organically, we would see the rise of Thrift Store Paintings.

Folk Art is essentially an untutored composite of found images and meaningful subjects produced for a local audience, usually for little or no money, made for pleasure and not shared outside of a narrow geographical area. It is detached from fine art, as it is not made with the expectation of wider cultural reception nor is it tied to the conventions of high culture. In the age of the time-lapse videos of artists creating a giant photorealist drawing of a lion's head or a trompe l'oeil glass of water (videos distributed instantly and universally on the Internet), where is the space for an artist to grow up ignorant of Western artistic conventions of proficiency? Why should today's Folk Art look anything like the seascapes of Alfred Wallis? How could it? In truth—as I noted in my article on Nikos Pirosmani—Folk Art has always been contaminated by mechanically reproduced images, from playbills to penny papers and banknotes. True isolation, if it ever was, is no longer feasible in an Internet age.

This is the crisis of localism. Localism is an approach which many people (including myself) have championed as an antidote to globalism and the proliferation of State Art production. If localism were to gain ascendancy, we would get a tidal wave of dreck, more modern than ancient. There would be more Cardi B than King Arthur, more memes than Medievalism, more nostalgia for Wimpy than wassailing. Demographic change, cultural depletion, expansion of Americanism and the hijacking of national symbolism have been so complete that any opening up of culture will likely result in an art (undirected by an elite) consisting of a broken vernacular of foreign pop culture and half-remembered liberal shibboleths. It would be an inadvertently Post-Modernist kind of Folk Art.

Folk Art is close to Bad Painting, a moniker which was coined in 1978 and a significant movement during the 1980s and 1990s. It is characterised by the intentional use by professional artists of devices, styles and content common to amateur and outsider art. The rise of this coincides with that of Post-Modernism and one can see Bad Painting as a strand within Post-Modernism's playful-cum-exploitative appropriation of other distinct artist lexicons. The difference between Folk Art and Bad Painting is self-awareness. Perhaps Bad Painting (as a canny, high-status variant of Folk Art) will become the national style in a decentralised national culture.

If we want artists to paint nature, we need to be teaching youngsters the difference between a chaffinch and a corncrake. At the moment more teenagers could give you a detailed break down of seasons of an anime show but couldn't tell you the difference between an oak and an ash. The groundwork for a new art based on local knowledge and pride has not been done. Today's artists who emulate Renaissance portraits have never worn a suit of armour nor handled a sword; perhaps they have never seen them in real life. I'm not arguing that we should return to an agrarian age and foreswear use of the Internet to make local art truly local. What I am arguing is that in the foreseeable future, our deracinated hybrid culture will (and already does) give rise to Folk Art that is full of pop culture, foreign influence, borrowed idioms and political banalities. Whether or not you find that prospect any worse than our current state, is a matter for your taste and convictions.

An art locked into a imperviously varnished Victorian historicism does not seem the product of a living culture but the product of a political stance. However much I might be sympathetic to the politics of traditionalists, I can't see historicism as a viable path for ambitious artists or a living culture. I appreciate a well-painted still-life as much as the next man but I need more than that. I don't know what I do want—outside of what I myself make—because I haven't yet seen it.

Localism may or may not undermine globalism but the art it will produce will range from the academic to Folk Art to Post-Modernism. Rest assured, like the art of most ages, much of it will be pretty bad. We will just have to hope that really great artists of tomorrow will find a way of making something original and powerful that speaks of its age and speaks to the ages. That said, localism may still be the best option available. Just be prepared for an outbreak of craft and some freshly made velvet Elvises.

13 May 2024

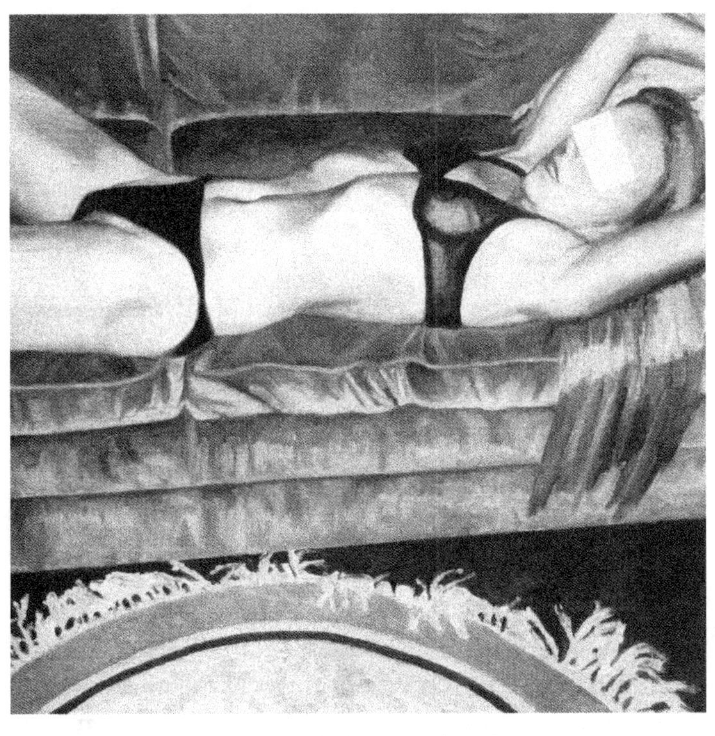

Alexander Adams, *Untitled* (c. 2003), oil on canvas, 16" x 16"/40 x 40cm

TEN

THE FUTURE IS NOT TRAD

Since I began publishing statements and articles, I have defended many forms of art. Operating on the basis that I found pleasure in many things and considering that we benefit from plurality (after all, my earliest polemical position was opposing State Art monoculture) I consequently supported Modernism, traditional art, folk art, crafts, abstraction, religious art and even (sparingly) Post-Modernism. From a solely tactical point of view, a broad alliance against the State Art status quo was strategically advisable as well as amenable to my outlook. Yet I have had reservations about modern-day practitioners of each style, mostly to do with the quality of the art. Doubts have become too pressing to be ignored and they will be the substance of this article.

My doubt is about the viability of certain forms—or more precisely, certain attitudes—for the vital iteration of any physical culture. I have previously written about the natural propensity among creative outliers to take risks.[1] For me, risk-taking is essential for a vanguard. I write here for anyone who judges himself to be part of (or allied to) a new wave of art made by those opposed to the State Art

---

1   See "High Risk, High Reward"

status quo. Those of us sufficiently arrogant, disagreeable, assertive and bold (reckless) must embrace our destinies by accepting our propensity to take risks and compulsion to break new ground. For outliers of the right (that is, of the historical centre) that means confronting the division between the reactionary and the conservative. Both tendencies have weaknesses but this discussion will cover the conservative proclivity to embrace symbols and structures.

The trouble with wishing to revive a Renaissance/Baroque/Pre-Raphaelite era of culture is twofold. The first (and least important) is capacity through emulation; the second is an attachment to tradition-as-form.

Conservatives correctly identify a problem inherent in Modernism, globalism and materialistic culture of our time, namely the way it detaches us from rootedness in soil (place) and blood (kinship). This has a deracinating effect. Severance from pre-Modern culture makes us ignorant of both craft and the tradition whence craft sprang, distancing us from folk knowledge and a sense of faithfulness to our predecessors. Hence conservatives advocate returning to tradition and localism. In the article "Bad Painting, Folk Art and Localism" I pointed out that we are already so immersed in world pop culture that localism is no longer viable, unless we return to a pre-Modern age of technology. When artists advocating Classicism or Romanticism talk of returning to the core of art and rootedness, I look at their art and I cannot (within the formal properties of the art) identify the century or country of production. This has come about because the traditionalist artists are so detached from tradition that they can find it only in the art of other centuries and countries. This makes their art more rootless than Pop Art or Neo Geo, because at least those styles have a definite era.

The already existing separation from the tradition is exacerbated by deliberate obfuscation. You traditionalists select views without modern buildings; in your landscapes you replace motorways with fields, in a conscious repastoralisation. I understand this because I did it too when I was a young artist.[2] Why not do the reverse? If you abhor contemporary eco-politics, do not hide away in Samuel Palmer idylls but paint a landscape including a wind turbine. You effectively criticise most when you show the truth or invent a parable that tells the truth, rather than refuting by running away. Have the courage to confront what you oppose, then criticise it. We need artists who are brave; being competent is not enough. Painting safe pictures for a pre-existing set of collectors is no advance. Make art that through the sheer force of your vision and ability brings into existence a new group of collectors, a new genre, a new art movement. Paint as you wish but if you want to be great, heed this warning.

I do not say you cannot or should not paint keeping in mind art of the past but remember the necessity of becoming fully yourselves. Yes, as a young artist Bruegel followed Bosch and he was as great (or greater) than the artist he followed. True, but Bruegel only became great when he went beyond Bosch, when he broke free, when he formulated a new language to address different topics. It was through apprenticeship that he reached the status of a great master. The only master who counts is one who masters himself. Where do I see you, admirers of tradition, saying you wish to go beyond what you now practice? Display the ambition of a great man by saying you will go beyond what you have learnt. Leonardo da Vinci wrote, "It is a poor pupil who does not surpass his master." What would Leonardo have done if he had been content to remain a follower of Verrocchio? Only by swearing "I must surpass Van Eyck, Raphael and Rembrandt" will you have a chance of equalling them.

2   See "I'm No Old Master, nor are You"

Why can't the essential qualities you wish to advance be incorporated into an art style you originate, one that others will wish to imitate? Think of those who will come after you. No one wishes to imitate an imitator. No one aspires to follow a spear-carrier. They wish to follow a leader or (in exceptional cases) to become a leader. If you have qualities which are eternal you find a place by situating them in context that means something and has importance for your time. If you believe that craft and skill are neglected, apply those to subjects of today. I am not asking you to make pictures of portrait subjects holding mobile phones as a gimmick, but be able to be a portraitist who is not afraid of including the modern. Such touches will locate your art in time and place and give it the rootedness you crave.

As Evola advised, be in your time (because you must be) but be not of your time (because you ought not to be). You can observe and commentate your situation but try not to fall into the fallacies of your age. The uplifting can be an image of something you dislike, that makes you uncomfortable, that imprints itself on to your memory through brilliant aggression. Making an adequate pastiche of a Romantic landscape is a display of competent imitation, but it will win over no viewer with a dash of sublime force. No, not every picture can rise to that level but an imitator's art never does because the highest threshold it can reach is adequacy. There is no space for meaningful originality, let alone genius.

You may find the picture in this article squalid—a poor representation of the type of ennobling art we stand to produce. Perhaps it is squalid. But there is more vitality in this than in any fantasia after Titian or Ruisdael because it has the stuff of life about it. It forces you to consider what is important to you. It asks you if realism (and reality) is compatible with your viewpoint. It asks that you to consider this figure that is shown in a pose and situation that is not flattering and to consider why the subject allowed herself to be captured in a such photograph originally and why she might find this image "her best self" to put out into the world. What expectations does she have of a woman's attractiveness and appropriacy and why might we consider her to be degraded (or at least not advantageously presented) in this image? You must consider the question, does this image have any redeeming qualities? It presents modern life without celebrating or promoting modernity.

Unless you are as good as the masters you follow, your art will not endure as theirs has. If you think Classicism or Romanticism is the route to immortality then you have learnt the wrong lesson. The brilliance of the Old Masters carried through their art resided not the forms or idioms. It was not the advancement of a formula. To contend otherwise is academicism in a time when the academy accepts political collectivists advocating for Afro-Futurism. You won't be granted admission into the Royal Academy and (without constant multi-generational vigilance) your self-founded academies face an identical fate.

So, we come to the second problem of conservative artists, that is their attachment to forms instead of spirit.

The future of art is not traditionalism because tradition, as TS Eliot observed, is something that springs from a linkage of living culture from which serious makers cannot be detached. "Yet if the only form of tradition, of handing down, consisted in following the ways of the immediate generation before us in a blind or timid adherence to its successes, "tradition" should positively be discouraged." So wrote Eliot in 1919, in his seminal essay "Tradition and the Individual Talent". He argues that even a poet working in new ways is part of a tradition that infuses his work with meaning, in the same way his era does, regardless of whether or not he employs the forms and styles of his antecedents. As the great writer submits himself ever more to his material and works honestly within the idiom of his age, his work is transmuted and absorbed into the tradition. "What happens is a continual surrender of himself as he is at the moment to something which is more valuable. The progress of an artist is a continual self-sacrifice, a continual extinction of personality. There remains to define this process of depersonalisation and its relation to the sense of tradition. It is in this depersonalisation that art may be said to approach the condition of science." Tradition is a sequence of adjustments and absorptions of innovations. Therefore innovation is necessary and normal within a living tradition.

In other words, actual tradition can survive as tradition-in-spirit but not as tradition-as-form because forms will (more than becoming moribund) be appropriated and repurposed. Consider the British Union flag—once a symbol of imperialism and military might, now an insignia for multicultural acceptance and soft-power liberalism. A "British sterling pound" no longer means anything as a weight of gold and soon will be abolished as cash, to exist virtually as a digital number, yet it is still notionally and nominally "one British sterling pound". Consider the aforementioned academies and how they no longer serve art but the interests of those who scorn what was cherished by the founders of the academy. Traditionalism in that respect is open to subversion because it is synonymous (in the most superficial understanding) with loyalty to a symbol. If that symbol is not within your group's control then it will be appropriated for degradation and repurposing. Put no trust in symbols and institutions unless you trust yourself to repudiate those things when they become perverted. Unlike symbols, a culture's spirit and content—like the canon—are beyond the complete control of enemies. Some would say that this tradition-in-spirit is a bio-spirit that lives on even though the people's landscape, clothing and speech change. However, history teaches us no culture is immortal. Without *asabiyyah* civilisation declines and communal feeling dwindles until the people are broken apart, as Ibn Khaldun set out.

I want to work with artists of all types. If you disagree with my reservations, exhibit beside me, outpaint me, make art that overcomes my reservations by being too astonishing to reject. Do not seek to be compared to any artist, no matter how great. Simply make pictures or sculpture that stands in and for itself, so alive that it seems more vivid than mere "art". Something that, as Paul Klee said, could come alive and threaten its creator. Make something that could live. When making art, aspire to not art but life.

Postscript

One of the dangers of an attachment to form over content, which might lead an anti-liberal to seek solace in the traditional, is the temptation to mistake "the Trad" for "tradition". The Trad is a purely aesthetic stance that we find manifest as a signal of hipster detachment from the mainstream. It is characterised by assertively rejecting the forms and styles of the post-1966 era, when we see the mainstreaming of Black, Gay and Women's Liberation as planks of political, social and civic life in the West. This takes the form of wearing clothing from earlier eras, listening to music on vinyl records and the rejection of many overtly modern devices and attitudes.

While some of Trad activity and signalling might be commendable or pleasurable in itself for participants, it is essentially a stance or a lifestyle, not a moral, intellectual or philosophical position. When asked why they have adopted this highly self-conscious position, participants talk in terms of liking the retro and appreciating the slow life (contra the high-turnover, fast-fashion attitudes of today).

There might be comments about having fond memories of their grandparents' life stories or possessions. There is a vague but strong conviction that "life was better then." Yet, if one were to put to the follower of the Trad lifestyle the proposition that the problem is not urban rap culture, smartphones, cryptocurrency, MP3 music files and unrepairable consumer goods but actually the ideas that underpin the society which produce such manifestations then one would draw uneasy glances. In other words, put to a Trad that the fundamental problems worth rebelling against are the notions that equality is normal and enforceable, that democracy is a compassionate and transparent form of government and that liberation movements (whose trappings they reject unspoken) were a determined assault on the natural order, one will be met by demurral.

Trad is the mildest conservativism, demonstrating a commitment to preserving and celebrating the shells of only-just-passed innovations, complete with every political prior that gave birth to those innovations, while at the same time believing one is the heir to ancient civilisation. It is only the digital age where he draws the line, yet he could not give up using a biometric passport to board a computer-flown jet to hear his favourite quasi-folk band play at Austin Music Festival. Trad is a sentimental attachment to the most convenient and obvious of outward appearances that signal a modest step back from the mainstream but only at a superficial level. To mistake a Trad position as implying comprehension of, or attachment to, deep-seated tradition is folly. Trad is part of the complex of poorly-thought-through attachments to forms moribund and materialistic, one we find present in the patriotism of Anglo-Futurism, the faith in localism as a counter to universalism and the championing of late-Nineteenth Century Arts and Crafts as a Gothic pre-Christian primitive sensibility.

We should not mistake Trad for Tradition. Although it may seem uncharitable to compare the Trad hipster aesthetic to the conservative's suggestion that Renaissance painting may be a viable contemporary art idiom, the two share the same wellspring mentality. The Trad and conservative think that if we can immerse ourselves in the past, our ancestors' world will arise up anew, somehow fusing ancestral sensibility with all the appurtenances of modern technology (as advocated by the Anglo-Futurists). This seems unlikely if the basic values held today differ so radically from those held by the great men of Western history and even by our relatives of a century past, as set out in these essays.

18 April 2025; postscript 16 June 2025

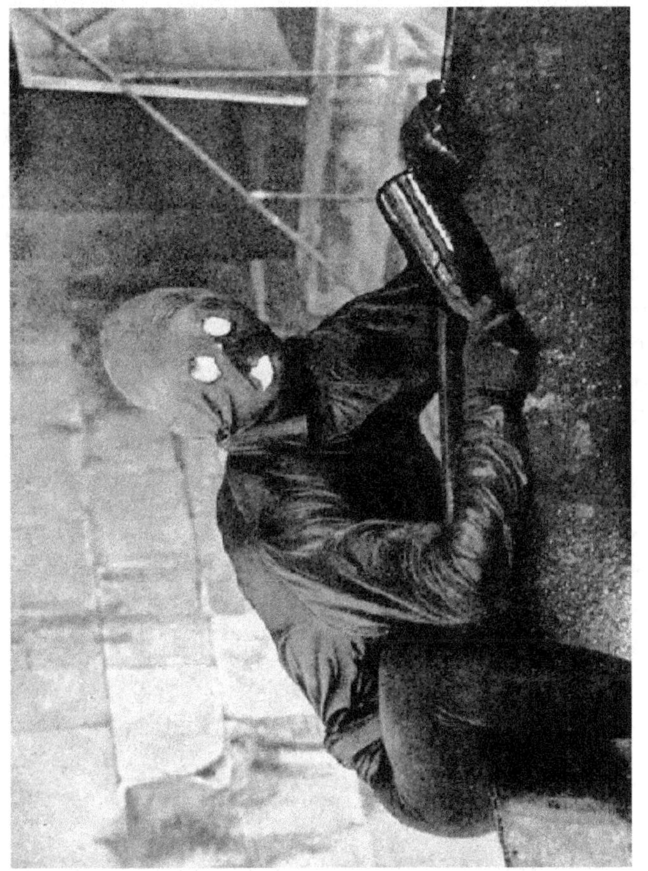

Fantômas, master criminal, 1913

ELEVEN

VIR HEROICUS SUBLIMIS

In my novel *The Naked Spur*, we encounter a protagonist who is freeing himself from the world. He leaves the gallery scene, he detaches himself from friends, he cuts himself off from the world gradually, talking to fewer people each day. He becomes a hermit and a recluse, who cannot bear to see people functioning, earning a living, enjoying life, even as his tentative yearning for intimacy is cut off and his aspirations of making art that will shake the world dwindle to naught. Although we do not see it directly in the novel, that character (named "A.") is the product of elite training. He studied at the best fine-art university department in the world. He rubbed shoulders with future stars of the art world; his tutors were rich and lauded. A. had every right to expect that if he was original and determined, he could sit at the high table beside them. He believed in the art world and the framework of meritocracy laid to his generation of future top-tier artists. *The Naked Spur* is the documentation of his decline into isolation, poverty and desperation due to his clinging to the story he was told as a young artist. The novel is an account of his brutal education and his inevitable extinction.

I recently re-read B.S. Johnson's novel *Christie Malry's Double-Entry* (1973). It is the story of a young accountant in London who becomes disaffected by his experience of life.

He resents the boredom of his routine and begins to fixate on injustice. He sees low-character individuals around him benefitting from the system and the talented poor missing out on opportunities due to poverty, lack of education and systemic class prejudice. Growing ever more alienated by a system that seems designed to perpetuate unfair and unjust outcomes—locked in place by corruption, indifference and snobbery—Malry begins to calculate recompenses. When he is inconvenienced by the placement of a wall, he scratches it. When a colleague angers him, he destroys a business letter which puts his colleague in an unfavourable situation. He starts to write a list of entries of debits (injustices, annoyances, injuries) against corresponding credits (discomforting, disrupting, sabotaging). Malry becomes a rebel and then, as things escalate, a terrorist. His campaign culminates in an act of mass murder.

In one internal monologue, Malry declares, "I am a cell of one". He understands himself as a isolated man, a hero (in his eyes) acting to wreak revenge for those too weak, stupid or afraid to act themselves. Malry is a "lone wolf" without affiliation, much less the aid of any fellow travellers. I was struck by the parallels between Malry and A. Both have potential. They have been compliant individuals and have sought to follow the systems they are raised within. They are not natural rebels. In some ways they are conformists who become deformed by the disillusionment they experience. They are not altruistic and act mainly to satisfy their emotional needs—in Malry's case by imposing his morality on wrongdoers, in A.'s case by attempting to become a successful artist. They gradually change from being passive to active, responding to circumstances by becoming more stubborn and extreme.

In *The Naked Spur* we see A.'s activities trying to set up a scheme that will allow him to operate as an anonymous artist (intending to make a living by selling nude paintings) intercut with news reports on the killings of the Beltway Killer, active in October 2002. Although it was not known until the arrest, the killer was actually a pair of men working together on their scheme to terrorise Washington DC, Maryland and Virginia with a series of random shootings in public. We see A.'s collaboration with Mack (complete with games of subterfuge, media manipulation and misleading rumours) as an unconscious parallel to the criminal acts of the Beltway Killer pair.

The *Vir Heroicus Sublimis* (Latin: man heroic and sublime) is embodied today in two figures: the artist and the criminal. Both are isolated, driven by ego and the overweening drive to impose their will on the world. They do not always want to claim credit publicly but they savour their triumphs. They are ultimately selfish and self-motivated. They seek to evade limitations imposed by society on the common man by acts of exceptional ability. They are brave, arrogant, intelligent, disagreeable, driven. Fundamentally unreasonable, they take risks at a level that most consider unwise, irrational, even insane. They operate outside the constraints of taste and decency; they scorn acceptance and mediocrity. Indeed, they prefer death to the dishonour of normality. They would rather fail than conform. Ultimately self-destructive, they would rather have their mental schema collapse and become discredited than see it compromised by the influence of society.

The Surrealists saw the analogy between the revolutionary artist and the criminal. Magritte had an affinity with the sinister character Fantomas, the supernatural anti-hero who appeared in detective stories and films, and whom he depicted in his art on a few occasions. Magritte clearly identified with the outlaw who defied both the laws of society and of nature.[1]

---

1   On the Surrealists support of violent criminality see Alexan-

In Nietzsche's conception, the artist is one archetype of the vanguard, who is entrusted as lawgiver and pathfinder. (The other is the warrior.) The pioneer artist is cursed to be misunderstood, like the prophet Zarathustra, who isolates himself on the mountaintop. Both are mocked and shunned. We can immediately see this exemplified in the career of Van Gogh. He is berated by his father as a heretic when he preaches the social gospel of Christ and is subsequently cast out of his Church. The accursed genius seeks solace among tragic prostitutes and unclean miners, only to be rejected by even them. With a religious fervour, Van Gogh pursues his calling to create a new art and bind together bands of brother-artists, expecting nothing but lifetime scorn followed by posthumous love. Van Gogh's self-written story is of a masochistic criminal-artist, living on the edge, courting rejection as much as seeking acceptance, unshakeable in his ecstatic egotism.

A. buys his materials from an art store on Commercial Street, close to the sites of the Jack the Ripper killings of 1888. Jack the Ripper is considered the archetype of the master criminal—a man of vicious sadism, unwilling (or unable) to stop outraging decency and the public peace in pursuit of his insatiable *Mordlust*. A. walks the streets of this killer in his activity as an artist—his own scheme to impose his will upon the world which seems determined to stymie him, when it is not a world entirely indifferent to his exceptional qualities. Unconsciously, A. begins to fall into the pattern of a serial killer or a terrorist. Yet, unlike a terrorist, he has no real cause and no external locus of resentment. Closer to a serial offender than artist, A. is brave but only so in private and eschews the lofty goals of the idealistic terrorist. We might think of A. as a misfit with

der Adams, *Women and Art: A Post-Feminist View*, Academia Press, Washington, 2022, pp. 59-66.

a grudge against society, yet rather than being in a single bedroom making bombs to blow up train carriages or politicians' homes, he is painting explosive pictures intended to bring down Bond Street and Cork Street galleries' paintings of conventional nudes. Rather than obliterating himself literally with a botched explosive device, the novel ends with A. obliterating his confidence and material circumstances through his incompetence.

There is veneration for the criminal and artist at the highest level (and a commensurate contempt for them at their lower levels of ability) because of their bravery and egotism. They engender a widespread lingering fascination with both their actions and their pathology, with a concentration on explaining their abnormalities through psychologising and sociological reading of their circumstances. Although one might assume that this fascination with the exceptionality of the artist and the criminal has two fixed moral polarities—we want to understand the brilliant artist because we need to identify his qualities and emulate his type of achievements and we want to understand the depraved criminal because we need to identify his morbidities and prevent his type of lawbreaking—we often find this is a grey area, where the criminal is lionised and the artist demonised. For every patrician art critic praising the radical artist, we have a scandalised conservative decrying the abasement of beauty and convention that this overrated shyster perpetrated. For every forensic psychologist alarmed at the imbalance of a killer, we have a hybristophiliac woman writing love letters to the gaoled murderer. The clarity of values and responses is not as clear as one might suppose or hope.

As that comment suggests, I do not say we should unthinkingly venerate either the artist or the criminal. The artist may be the way-finder for an ideological faction that is devasting to us. Through neophilia, counter-elite backing and zealous passion, the artist may open horrors and be an agent for chaos that destroys what we love and need. He may be the tool for those seeking to undermine a culture. I do not see creativity as valuable in itself and I do not see the artist as above common morals. The unfortunate fact is that for the artist to be the exceptional individual, he breaks conventions and laws and must have the determination to fight his cause, although that will cause suffering to others and himself. Beware the believer, for he might do what we conventionally claim to want but always expect never to be enacted.

Unlike Malry, A. is part of a disenfranchised elite, a surplus who is unable to compete because of the overproduction of the elite-tier artists through an art-education system that is the victim of its own success and was in the process of a down cycle, marked by excess of prospective professional artists and the decline in quality of artists and art. Pareto states in his treatise on elite theory, that in order for a system to function, there must be an adequate supply of elites in order to allow the cycling of competent individuals for the system to thrive. The less competent are replaced by the more competent, with competition directing individuals, improving practice and causing the system to gain in efficiency. If there are too few suitable individuals then the technocratic society suffers inefficient management, corruption flourishes, society grows mistrustful of the elite. The danger of the overproduction of the elite is that there arises a critical mass of disaffected, intelligent, qualified, motivated individuals who cannot gain entry into a sufficiently high level of the system. This forms into an organised minority (as per Mosca) which co-ordinates and agitates and—if a cycle of entry and release is not made available—foments not only discontent but revolt. This is a counter elite. We see such an elite forming today. A. was part of the Generation X elite trained in the early/mid-

1990s, many of whom (in the 2000s) were denied entry into the upper stratum of fine art, namely the self-supporting fine artists. Thus, A. was fated to be part of the nascent counter-elite. We must admit that A.'s behaviour, characteristics and aesthetic affiliations certainly contribute to his failure to gain a stable foothold in the art world that had been (if not promised then) offered him by the system. Come the 2010s, such artists were permanently locked out of the usual route of advancement through Arts Council funding, regional venues, art competitions, prizes, scholarships, teaching positions and museum-and-state patronage, which were now allocated mainly on political or demographic markers. If we want a social explanation for the dissident cultural scene, we have it there in an elite-theory nutshell.

Yes, all very pat. In this explanation, we overlook A.'s wilful deviance. If he wanted advancement, all A. had to do was conform by producing art that could be commissioned by the state. This was the course taken by colleagues who were cycled into the system, making art to fit commissioning briefs with which the artists had no meaningful engagement and no deep understanding. Artists less talented than A. made comfortable careers by adopting and reflecting the politics of the regime, finding ways of translating into art mantras of establishment ideology, in forms subtle to blatant. They put themselves in the service of the participatory art event and the therapeutic agenda of the museum-as-social-hub. In short, we cannot attribute A.'s failure entirely to his situation as a member of the surplus elite but rather to a conscious drive to resist acceptance on the terms set out by the art establishment. It is the criminal's urge to defy authority—or to seek personal gratification disregarding the prevalent norms—that we see in A. and Malry. When Johnson has Malry say "I am a cell of one" he gets his protagonist to state his position as both a dedicated agent of disruption but also an atomised individual, without power to effect lasting change because he acts alone. Both characters are victims of their naivety, expecting the world to be governed by fairness not by power, and who slowly come to realise their folly.

In his own way, Malry is an failed artist and A. is a failed criminal. Such is the fate of many of us.

16 May 2025

TWELVE

GREEN SUNS AND CYBER-CATHEDRALS:
ON NATIONAL FUTURISM

Not right, not left, forwards: Transcending outdated divisions to cultivate future-centric, civilisational politics, unbound by legacy factions.

Anglo-Futurist slogan, 26 June 2025

I

In the run-up to receiving the book under discussion in this article, I fortuitously encountered (quite at random) a Japanese art manifesto. Written in 1910 by Takamura Kōtarō, the short manifesto "Green Suns" sets out the question of whether a Japanese can integrate Western art style and remain authentically Japanese. It will have some bearing on the issue under discussion. Artist Kōtarō describes how he views himself in relation to the European art he has been influenced by.

> I am born Japanese. Just as a fish can't live out of water, so I can't live as a non-Japanese, even if I remain quiet about it. At the same time, just as a fish isn't conscious that he's wet in the water, so at times I am not conscious that I'm Japanese. 'At times' isn't the right expression. I'm more often unconscious than not. I often think I'm Japanese when I'm dealing with someone. The thought doesn't occur much when I face nature. That is, I think of it when

> I think of my own turf. Such a thought can't possibly occur when I have my own self thrown an object.
>
> My psychological state while making art is, therefore, where only one human being exists. Thoughts of things like Japan don't exist at all. I simply go ahead, thinking, seeing and feeling as I do, regardless. The work, when you look at it later, may turn out to be so-called Japanesey. It may not. Either way, it won't bother me, the artist, at all. Even the existence of local colour, in such an instance, will mean nothing.[1]

Kōtarō argues that because the artist is Japanese, he does not need to bow to pressure of making things Japanese because everything he does must be Japanese. "No matter how non-Japanese, a work made by a Japanese can't avoid being Japanese."[2] Therefore, if a Japanese artist (under the influence of French Impressionism or Post-Impressionism) paints a green sun, Kōtarō will not condemn him as un-Japanese. This argument seems the standard case for individualism, arguing that enculturation means any individual's actions are an expression of his culture; therefore by pursuing individual freedom of expression, national character cannot be weakened. It resides within the individual personally as well as in the group collectively. However, this manifesto was written at a time before the permeation of societies with highly complex, perfectly replicable, digitally transmitted cultural material of foreign origin. The most obvious objection to Kōtarō is that such attitudes for artists only work at an individual (not social) level and as an exception. Scaling up Kōtarō's proposition creates a problem regarding widespread non-conformity and consequent dilution of culture, especially in the face of concerted liberal political pressure to de-nature nation-

---

1   Takamura Kōtarō, "A Green Sun", 1910, in Alex Danchev (ed.), 100 Artists' Manifestos, Penguin, London, 2011, p. 21.
2   Ibid., p. 23.

al character. What might be a tolerable exception for a handful of creative individuals cannot be effected broadly without weakening national independence.

> I'd like the artist to forget that he's Japanese. I'd like him to rid himself entirely of the idea that he is reproducing nature in Japan. And I'd like him to express on his canvas the tone of nature as he sees it, freely, indulgently, wilfully. [...] An appreciator [...] should simply recognize [this art] is different, and then try to see on the basis of the work whether the artist's sentiments are based on something false or on his innate sincerity. The goodness or badness of the work must come into his mind as a separate issue.[3]

This passage suggests that innate national character will inevitably emerge with the artist making a conscious effort. This very issue of conscious embodiment of national character in the pursuit of creative endeavours (individual and group) is at the core of the current debate—one hundred years after Kōtarō's "Green Suns"—on National Futurism (NF) of both Anglo and American strands. If you have paid attention to the art press over the last decade you will have heard about collectives promoting Afro-Futurism. The fact we in the West are more accustomed to hearing of the African variant than the English or American ones tells you more about the interests of our art press than it does about the recent trajectory of art.

NF presents itself as a workable solution to the identity issue afflicting Western culture. It offers itself as the answer to this question: How can nations retain their culture in an age of multicultural pressure, mass migration and technologically driven globalisation? It gives a framework that should not scare off too many people, offers a nationalism that is not proscriptively trad and advances an urbane alternative to the primal (sometimes bleak) visions

---

3   Ibid., p. 22.

of vitalists sceptical of technology.

But what if that very reasonableness betrays NF's artificial character and masks a deeper unsoundness?

II

Before approaching the subject of the new National Futurist movements, I should add a disclaimer. I am on friendly terms with Rachel Haywire, the National Futurist Party (an association of likeminded creatives, not actually a political/legal entity) and Fiume Gallery, New York. Author Alexander D'Albini kindly answered my questions to him about Anglo-Futurism, for which I am grateful. So, I am naturally well disposed towards the people whose ideas I shall be critiquing. I have admiration for those who are inventive and thoughtful individuals who reject liberalism and who also find their outlook incompatible with religious or social conservatism. However, I have for years made clear that I think that a fundamentally materialist reading of history—and any consequent basing of personal/social principles upon humanism—is problematic, without being able to suggest a satisfactory alternative course.

That done, let us look at what NF claims it is and what it offers.

In *Collected Essays on AngloFuturism Philosophy* Alexander D'Albini sets out of the principles of the movement in a collection of essays written in the second half of 2024. Anglo-Futurism (AF) is the traditions of the Anglo people and the technology of futurism. The five pillars of AF are family, housing, order, technology and competency.[4] D'Albini considers AF to be an antidote to "ten spectres of the Anglosphere", which he identifies as Digital Addiction, Social Comparison, Cyber-Aggression, Overconsumption,

4   Ibid., p. 6.

Environmental Neglect, Isolation and Dehumanisation, Apathy, Cultural Erosion, Surveillance Overreach, and Technological Hubris.

This malaise was summarised in more concrete terms by Aris Roussinos in a 2022 article.

> The fundamental problem facing Britain today is the collapse of this chosen model, the fruit of a previous, lesser era of crisis. Instead of shoring up the state's resilience to the pressures of an increasingly unstable world, the reliance on market forces has left the Government increasingly unable to impose order, provide functioning healthcare, keep the lights on or put roofs over people's heads: a state that cannot provide these basic functions is really no state at all.[5]

The British state, paralysed by incompetent short-termism in the service of uniparty functionaries, is spiralling downwards in uncontrolled decline. What is needed for British potential to be unlocked is a revolutionary hyper-competent technocracy.

> It is a country where cheap and reliable high-speed rail darts across the country, through the new towns where everyone who wants can have their own warm and spacious home, past the small family farms which provide the country's food security. In the clean skies, electric airships move freight across the country.[6]

In his book D'Albini's sets out the basic position of AF. "AngloFuturism is not socialist, not progressive, nor conservative, or nationalist. It is Anglo."[7] As D'Albini's definition of Anglo means of the culture of the people who came from the British Isles—so that it can include not just

---

5   Aris Roussinos, "It's Time for Anglofuturism", *UnHerd*, 29 August 2022. https://unherd.com/2022/08/its-time-for-anglofuturism/
6   Ibid.
7   Alexander D'Albini, *Collected Essays on AngloFuturism Philosophy*, self-published, Great Britain, December 2024, p. 5.

Great Britain but the former colonies of the USA, Canada, Australia and New Zealand—he cannot say that English or British nationalism is the priority, as this would relegate the Anglo diaspora to secondary status and complicate the aims of AF. Anglo ethnos is fairly easy to define, although the edges may be fuzzy. We can straightforwardly describe the ethnic English as descendants of the ancient British peoples, plus Romans, Angles, Saxons, Normans and Vikings.

The definition of AF's "Anglo" is not ethnically British and born in Great Britain but rather what Anglos decide is part of their Anglo tribe; this may (or may not) include British/English ancestry but should not include everyone of that ethnos; this is because (according to AF) Anglo is ethos as well as ethnos. "The 'spirit of the Anglo' is the defining criteria to being an Anglo."[8] What is "the spirit of the Anglo"? D'Albini nominates respect for tradition, collective wisdom, common sense, optimism, inventiveness, moderation, practicality and spirituality. The author has a Christian faith and sees its importance for Anglo society but he does not specify Christianity as a bedrock for a revived Great Britain. Communitarian spirit is a necessity, writes D'Albini.

AF rejects ethno-nationalism because not all ethnically associated Anglo people share Anglo values, whereas ethnically non-Anglo people may share Anglo values. D'Albini suggests that Anglos are not self-defined, yet he adds "anyone can align with Anglo culture as long as they embody its Spirit."[9] That seems a circular definition: an Anglo (or Anglo ally) is someone who defines himself as Anglo. It is also problematic. D'Albini writes that an ethnic Anglo who denies his culture can be treated as non-Anglo, which

8   Ibid., p. 73.
9   Private letter by D'Albini to Adams, 3 July 2025.

could give rise to the situation of a first-generation Indian admonishing an ethnic Englishman that it is he, the Indian, who is the truer Anglo.

A century ago the definition of "Anglo" would have been Christian (devout or nominal), born of old English stock, English speaking, martial, suspicious of the foreigner and devoted to king, country, God and family. It would have been not primarily a matter of choice but one of birth. This has been completely inverted, so that today a British person is defined by "modern British values", which are multiculturalism, cosmopolitanism, individualism, democracy and tolerance; most importantly, it means ascribing to such values, regardless of one's religion, ethnicity, language and place of origin. In other words, for the British state "a British subject" means anyone who complies with the state's values and has British residency (not even citizenship); "Anglo" is an anachronism, with distasteful undertones. AF eschews "modern British values" but it fights shy of embracing the older definition, noting that touchstones change over time. D'Albini claims AF is not civic-nationalism, as civic-nationalism is top-down, state-imposed and "too abstract". Yet I am unpersuaded that in either theoretical or practical terms AF is distinguishable from civic-nationalism.

NF is particularist in that it favours the domestic over the foreign and clearly supports the drive to discriminate on the basis of national self-interest. This suggests it is aligned with the insights of elite theory. On the other hand, D'Albini's AF advocates a form of governance based upon the English disposition towards operating in small co-operative units based on clans, guilds and villages. Although this might lend itself to feudalism, D'Albini suggests that for Anglos democracy is both possible and admirable, something at odds with elite-theory insight, which states oligarchy is the natural form of all governance in developed societies. Democracy is used as a veil to conceal from the population the true nature of power, which is top down. D'Albini has written elsewhere that he is supportive of the principle of monarchy. American NF appears a lot more open to autocracy and less wedded to democracy.

From a nationalist perspective, AF can be criticised in two respects outside of the ethnos issue. The first is that AF is managerial in character. AF could claim that managerialism is the misplaced prioritisation of the permanent managerial elite of the task of directing elements within the state for purposes of that cadre's own continuation. In other words, managers maintain a system for their own benefit, with the welfare of the nation, land and national values a secondary consideration; sometimes even opposing to those three non-state aspects when they conflict with the security and power of the managerial elite. AF aims to reverse that hierarchy, thereby dissolving the "managerialist ethos" whilst preserving its structures and even personnel, needed for advanced technical projects, such as land reclamation from the sea (Doggerland) and space exploration.

Without a working example of a present-day NF state in the West, we have no evidence of the viable application in practice of such an ethos-driven national management system.[10] Theoretically, such a system might be an improvement on our current plight but familiarity with Michels's Iron Law of Oligarchy suggests that any complex system of managerialism must serve itself. NF seems an optimistic shot at incentivising a streamlined civil service staffed by patriotic managers, ones willing to abolish their own departments and make themselves redundant. NF has acknowledged the problem of a parasitical permanent

10   We might describe the non-Western states of Russia and China as paradigms of the autocratic isolationist nationalist state.

civil service in a complex industrial society, has seen that a reordering of values is needed to combat this system's self-serving nature, but has failed to outline a means of changing values.

The second nationalist criticism is that NF is at heart an acquiescence to technocracy, which tends towards social atomisation. D'Albini claims techno-nationalism is the route to utilitarianism; AF is a transnational project and acknowledges that suffering and community are a part of human experience, therefore it is different from techno-nationalism. While D'Albini's essays seem to assume that technology can serve aspects such as family, community and nationhood, it is hard to see how any society that venerates technology would be able to reliably retain this hierarchy. After all, we have not. Technology has divided family members in individual cocoons of technological engagement. It is hard to see how much would change in an AF-dominated country, as we already run society as a compromise between tradition and technology.

AF is avowedly "non-political and non-nationalist"[11] and accepts "Anglo ethos" *in toto*, so it cannot help but seem technical and aesthetic in nature. The unofficial symbol of AF is the red squirrel, which represents native British inhabitants. This is implicitly counterposed with the immigrant grey squirrel population, which has almost entirely displaced the native species in many places in mainland Britain. Contrast the AF red squirrel with the American NF's eclectic preferences for Roman statuary, punk imagery, Goth aesthetics and neon graphics. While the cottage is commonplace in AF memes, Americans eschew the log cabin, instead adopting the space rocket. The aesthetic difference is telling. AF is (despite AFs' protestations) pastoral and backwards looking; American NF

---

11   D'Albini, 2024, p. 21.

is metropolitan and forwards looking. National character shines through in the two NFs' imagery.

Nationalists would conclude that to save the Anglo project it is necessary to save the Anglo ethnos. AF's reluctance to address this betrays liberalist priors. Anything that liberals might consider taboo has not been broached by AF. My question to AFs is—aside from questions of values—how serious are you about protecting Anglo people? Any group in a territory will be surrounded by competitor nations and supra-national organisations intent on implementing globalisation. So, what is the response of AF, other than navigating to the best advantage of the Anglo people on an issue-by-issue basis? Without assertive nationalism to defend the homeland and prevent subversion, how can AFs achieve any of their goals?

Do AFs think Anglo values can survive the absence of the Anglo people? If so, then the Anglo population is superfluous and globalism can be adjusted to reflect the Anglo-cultural memeplex without the existence of the Anglo population. If not, then is AF willing to advocate strong measures to protect the Anglo ethnos (demos)?

If AF has a future it needs to become bolder and more emotional. Anglo compromise and politeness has contributed to the parlous state of Great Britain. AF's determinedly apolitical position means it is not well situated as a vehicle for social defence, which would require base emotions to motivate discrete campaigns on specific issues. AF gives inspiration and purpose and suggests areas for improvement, but expects technology to provide the tools necessary for solutions and for others to direct the action. I understand that if the AF writers see themselves as thinkers and inspirers, they would be reluctant to commit themselves to setting out a political platform. (By disavowing politics, they have ruled themselves out of policy setting.) Therein lies the problem. By taking us to the point of policy formation and then handing over responsibility to others, AF followers will inevitably drift towards existing wings of the uniparty that have already demonstrated their inadequacy.[12] In saying AF is a platform which any political party can adopt, AFs allow their vision to be deceptively appropriated by pre-existing organisations which caused the very problems AF opposes.

On balance, AF is a creditable project but I fear that new technology, good will and "British values" may not take us far as the advocates of Anglo-Futurism hope.

III

When it comes to the American National Futurism (ANF), the appearance and vibes are very different. Where AF is cosy, ANF is edgy. Dark-synth soundtracks, industrial rock, military imagery, Goth clothing, uncompromising nudity and Brutalist architecture dominates ANF social-media posting and cultural events. There is energy, urgency, excitement; we are left with the impression that this is a movement that is prepared to confront the dangerous and unpleasant. ANF is closer than AF to the live wire of vitalism, which disrupts settled styles and rote responses. ANF is not out to reassure and is not disposed to produce travel posters in the 1925 style. ANF is liable to make itself awkward but not for the sake of it, but because personal expression is more important than consensus. We could draw analogies between ANF in 2025 with the nascent scenes of Abstract Expressionist in 1940 and Trans-Avant-Garde in 1980. All three movements share New York as a locus.

In centralised, big-state Great Britain, AF looks for provision of state-directed essential services and the opening

---

12   There was excitement in AF circles in June 2025 when leading Conservative Party politician Robert Jenrick declared himself to be an Anglo-Futurist.

up of regulation to allow science and industry to provide solutions. In federal, small-state USA, ANF wants to gather and unleash artistic-entrepreneurial creativity in an anarchic cultural tsunami, driven by and for the people—but only the sharpest, smartest, most ambitious of individuals. The Americans have sharper elbows and are less worried about perturbing colleagues or the general public. A telling note is that while AF often speaks about the Anglosphere and joint efforts benefitting Anglo-originated societies, ANF is out for the USA; the Anglosphere hardly gets mentioned. One is irresistibly reminded of the imbalance found in the British concept of the "special relationship" between Britain and the USA in the post-1945 international geo-politics; this was a myth of no substance (certainly not after the Suez Crisis) but it was one that the British elite caste told itself to reassure them that they were respected and influential; Americans indulged it as an advantageous delusion. No one in the ANF movement will be swapping out their "Make America Great Again" baseball caps for "Make the Anglosphere Great Again" ones.

ANF sidesteps religious and sexual standards and fixes upon less contentious areas that have high social capital, ones that can be approached by those of any political persuasion, namely art, architecture, social organisation, urban planning, transport—all areas that might benefit from the application of new technological tools. ANF does not have a strict moral code that would scare away libertines, homosexuals and transsexuals. ANFs are goths, punks, clubbers, bikers, hipsters, slam poets, scene liggers. ANF will not force you into an ankle-length dress or laser off your tattoos. Rather than take away your Xanax and Vyvance, your cannabis and cocaine, you will be invited to consider if your narcotic consumption detracts from the welfare of your compatriots or compromises your health.

An absence of distinct moral code and social amenability courts the accusation of ANF that it is opportunistic and insincere. American cultural commentator Dave Greene has developed a critique of ANF in "The Rise of the LinkedIn Right"[13], which I recommend to anyone interested in this subject. Greene states ANF is an countercultural project dressed up as national revivalism. Underlying Greene's criticism is a view that materialism and humanism are unmoored and therefore prone to being diverted into utilitarianism. Without a sense that societies benefit from spiritual unity of ethos and ethnos (disconnected from prosperity) mere political positioning opens the door to misplaced loyalties, opportunism and exploitation. The worldview (which Greene calls "the New Secular Right" (NSR)) seems contingent and not deep rooted. It is difficult to imagine anyone feeling strongly enough to fight or die for this cause.

Greene writes, "The perspective never seems to fit together since the NSR worldview always comes off like it was crafted by a marketing focus group rather than organically evolving from experience or first principle." NSR/ANF seems like a project founded on the calculation that technocrats' attachment to competence would make them agreeable towards a rebranded liberalism—liberalism cut free from anti-white and anti-national dogma, which tends to advance diversity candidates and policies that are both antithetical to competence. NSR/ANF makes no demands of potential allies or defectors from the ruling elite regarding private spirituality, sexual ethics, objective morality or ethnic solidarity. It takes no position on religion. NSR/ANF is post-religious and post-ethnic and therefore is untethered to age-old wellsprings of identity.

In other words, at its baldest, NSR/ANF appears cal-

13 https://fiddlersgreene.substack.com/p/the-rise-of-the-linke-din-right, Fiddler's Greene, Substack, 23 May 2024.

culated not felt. On the careerist character of the online NSR/ANF, Greene observes, "the New Secular Right feels exactly like modern anti-progressive ideas were forced through the LinkedIn meta-filter." It seems like something you could try out for a few seasons, all the while keeping your options open. It never requires you cut off anything or anyone of importance to you. It demands no wars, no tithes, no book-burning, no physical or emotional sobriety, not even personal penance. Maybe a few statues will need removing; streets and buildings will have to be renamed; a few egregious NGOs will have to be proscribed; a handful of civil servants will lose their jobs. ANF is reset rather than revolution.

Are agnostic ANFs supping with the Devil when they seek deals with Big Tech? ANFs bear comparison with the early adopters of technology. They are the first to have a microchip implanted in their hands and the last to realise that this novel concession to convenience is a shackle, able to restrict and detain as much as it permits access. Digital identities and currencies are sold on convenience and framed as horizon expansion but are always used to track and limit and (eventually) to control and punish. Approval of governments for technological innovation always includes the power to coerce the administrators of that technology to enact nudges for aims agreed by the governing elite. ANFs see technology as a potential liberator whereas grim experience leads many of us to consider innovation in technology less of a freeing-up of human potential and more an ever-narrowing chute leading sentient humans into an abattoir.

In my experience, ANFs are not naïve or reckless with regard to technology. They see technological routes as potentially fruitful creatively but they understand that focus on the medium is the road to aridity. They are also perfectly savvy about the dangers of patrons distorting or discarding

ANF if the movement proves obstreperous. They already have had personal contact with investors and collectors—they rub shoulders with them at the same parties and bars. ANF is in part realpolitik. If you are a counter-elite and you do not have the street muscle or guerilla army to force revolution, you try the reverse Long March Through the Institutions[14]. In this case, you bypass universities and political organisations and instead concentrate on winning over the ruling elites in industry to your exclusive art movement, offering the tech arm of the ruling elite a chance to trade up from Gay Pride to national pride and ditch Diversity Is Our Strength quotas for a meritocracy of inegalitarian achievers who don't care about being called racist (while at the same time being multi-racial, multi-faith, metropolitan-inhabiting, chilled-out social liberals). These are artists you can patronise but also ones you might consider hanging out with, without having to put up with tiresome social-justice cant and without fear of sexual-harassment suits.

The problem is that ANF's absence of moral framework and the casualness with which supporters have taken it up—as an investment that could go sour but ultimately is just a financial punt rather than a commitment—mean that (if patronage were to evaporate) the movement could dissolve without leaving a lasting cultural or political legacy. Without entry of people with different values into the ruling elite, ANF entryism (and influence) will remain superficial and limited to a few top-level cultural

14   The campaign set out by German socialist Rudi Dutschke in the late 1960s (inspired by Gramsci) which involved infiltrating national establishments at all levels through left-wing entryism in order to control organisations through subversion, activism and sabotage, obviating the need for armed insurrection or electoral victory.

producers, influencers and commentators. ANF's viability depends on its openness and heterogenous affect, which will attract vestigial liberals, anxious affluent types, the frustrated managerial caste and disaffected patricians, a rainbow coalition not so far from the progressive one, and one which has commitment that is a mile wide and an inch deep. If you want NF to really permeate the elite and reshape society you need a rise in instinctual separatism and oikophilia that is contra to liberalism's universalism and oikophobia. NF ethno-abstentionism is not going sufficiently distinguish itself in value terms to effect such a change. NF is essentially managerial, as it believes in re-directing the present elites by offering tangible incentives; nationalism requires profound commitment to ethnos (or demos), ethos and topos, which NF does not offer. What Greene does not mention is the difficulty of raising any sort of American movement in the modern USA based on race. We might consider ANF an attempt to prevent racial fragmentation of the state through the imposition of super-competency by a technocratic elite. ANF is the last chance for the USA to remain functioning and recognis-able. In that sense, there is a residual nostalgia that ANF shares with AF.

IV

So, what does NF offer artists and should NF be a banner under which dissident artists should gather? NF's eclectic character, aesthetic openness, acceptance of new media, rejection of off-the-shelf solutions, freedom of expression, fierce inegalitarianism and absence of academicist tenden-cies all recommend NF to the questing artist. All this sug-gests that NF is a suitable movement for assorted patriots, dissidents, outsiders and adventurous artists. The spirit of NF is exhilarating but NF aesthetics in themselves tend towards the cliché. NF's standbys of nostalgia, retro-tech and AI are dead ends to be avoided. As a sceptic of cultural nostalgia—or rather, recognising the allure of its pungent, soporific effect—I respond negatively towards AF's memes. Something more serious and substantial is called for if a stand is to be taken. AF is, after all, a self-conscious stand in itself. A revival of Art Deco, Futurism and Vorticism has been mooted as a potential artistic style for AF.

The directionlessness of NF aesthetics and absence of fixed core values—other than an acknowledgement of elite theory, valuing communitarian action and attachment to national self-interest (contra state interest)—means artists will have to search deeper within themselves to find the wellspring of a personal art, even if they find themselves coming together as National Futurists to share their discoveries.

If artists can take up the attitude and channels of NF then they have a good mid-point. If artists take NF as their starting point they risk getting mired in careerism or shallowness; if artists take NF as their destination then they have not achieved transcendence and immateriality that is the final point of all immortal art in its highest state.

Takamura Kōtarō, "A Green Sun" (1910), in Alex Danchev (*ed.*), *100 Artists' Manifestos*, Penguin, London, 2011

Alexander D'Albini, *Collected Essays on AngloFuturism Philosophy*, self-published, Great Britain, December 2024

Aris Roussinos, "It's Time for Anglofuturism", *UnHerd*, 29 August 2022

Dave Greene, "The Rise of the LinkedIn Right", *Fiddler's Greene*, Substack, 23 May 2024

10 July 2025

——

THIRTEEN

ART AS ATTRITION

Recently, a new statue erected in Times Square, New York attracted much comment, mostly negative. The overweight physique, slouching pose, truculent attitude, absence of any grace, energy or invention in the subject and treatment render this piece oppressively leaden—as well as horribly oversized. The use of digital scanning and enlargement makes the statue singularly characterless, lacking nuance and touch. The creator is British artist Thomas J Price, a black artist, whose primary works appear (even they might not actually be) scanned, 3D-printed and then cast in silicon bronze.

If it looks oddly familiar, you may be remembering Price's *Moments Contained* (2023), a 13-foot-high statue of a black woman standing with hands in her pockets, placed near the main train station of Rotterdam. This is not to be confused with *Reaching Out* (2020), a 9-foot tall statue of a black woman consulting her mobile phone, situated in a park in Stratford, London. Not to be confused with *Time Unfolding* (2025) a giant black woman consulting her phone, presented in the Piazza della Signoria, Florence. It goes one better than the (replica) Michelangelo David situated nearby, by being gilded.

If you research Price's output, you will find that this is the only thing he does: black people dressed casually, standing undemonstratively, often using mobile phones. Although some are modelled on actual individuals, the statues are always of anonymous characters. They are, in their way, archetypes; they are Platonic ideals of the Black Everyman and Everywoman (so described by *The Guardian*). They have no distinctive differences between each other, other than sex and body mass index. They are absolutely generic. Titles convey the sense of passivity and existence without purpose or role.

You may have felt dissatisfaction with Price's statues beyond scorning their absence of distinctive positive aesthetic attributes, while not being able to pin down the origin of your unease. This comes from a critical change made to the purpose of public statuary. The first public statues were of kings, appointed rulers, gods and mythological characters; later came figures of Christ, Mary and the saints; later were individuals of note, namely martyrs, nobility, generals, patrons and civic dignitaries. In the wake of the formation of nation states (where men fought for country as opposed to their lord) came statues commemorating the glorious fallen, as individuals or composite men. Then came statues of working men, made in the late Nineteenth Century. These reached their apogee in the capable hands of Belgian Constantin Meunier (1831-1905). His observations in sculpture were matters of human admiration and regional pride. These figures were not generic, although they were anonymous and non-specific. They excited admiration because they were masterfully observed and crafted depictions of workers (mainly men) who were admired for their fortitude, stamina, skill and dedication to difficult, skilled or dangerous tasks which benefitted all. They were portraits of crafts as much as the men themselves, although we see the anatomical alterations their use made to their bodies and the special poses and clothing unique to their occupations. It was (and is) amazing art and the product of diligence lavished on men whose qualities were valued by all.

It was inevitable that Meunier's statues would taken as a template for the Social Realism of his era and the Socialist Realism of the eras that followed. The brawny bare-chested miner and haggard stevedore of Eastern Europe city buildings and parks are Meunier's indirect offspring. Less dynamic, more maudlin examples of worker archetype are to be found in recent statues of the anonymous miner, agricultural labourer and foundry worker that are the staple of high streets of towns across our land. They have been erected by councils to honour trades and occupations that once provided the fulcrum for communities; the descendants of these workers now subsist on civil service jobs, teaching, shop work and government benefits. In a pedestrianised street overlooked by chain stores, cafés, charity shops, nail bars, vape shops and Turkish barbers, has been erected by the council a worthy-insipid bronze of a millhand beside a barefoot child worker. Arabs and Africans walk past indifferently; in the shadow of the statue group a gypsy has set out a stand of Chinese-made novelty toys.

Price's art has the banality of these legacy-industry archetypes but has a quite different meaning and intention. Price's everymen and everywomen are created to be admired because they were born black. They are shown in no pursuit or activity (other than vacant interaction with their mobile telephones). Public statuary has gone from specific heroes to members of certain jobs to generic ethnic tokens. We are supposed to notice Price's figures and accept them "for who they are" not for what they do. They seem to have no job, no role in society, no exceptional qualities, nothing distinctive other than the attributes they were born with. They exemplify the culture of reward for existence not for achievement. We must accept these statues and by inference their hymning of today's passive, leisure-focused, self-oriented existence. It is never suggested to us why we should admire or accept the figures or what they represent. The figures are there to be acknowledged for their sheer existence. As the artist himself said, "It is also about people being able to recognise themselves, or people they know." As occupation-free anonymous types, Price's figures are Marxist in their opposition to the Carlylean notion of proper-thinking men admiring great men for their achievements and taking them as heroic models; the New Statues imply that we are all worth immortality in statue form and that those great men (the generals, explorers and martyrs) are recipients of unearned advantages and not really so special after all. New Statues have shucked even the heroism of unknown labourers, soldiers or firemen; they are free of duties and suffering, raised to be respected for nothing.

Price's figures could—and have been—placed anywhere; no situation can change their register or meaning. (Instead they are used to change the sites.) The very isolated, atomised interiority of the statues' attitude is the purpose of them. Price says, this is the black everywoman and she is untouched by culture, location or nation; her presence is a sign of modernity; my sculpture is an assertion that she has as much claim to this space as your ancestors and heroes. The State Art nexus of the permanent managerial elite operating through civic bureaucracy, museum curation, art biennales, arts-sponsorship bodies, internationalist charities and a London West End gallery allows Price's statues to be acquired for your historical plaza, important train station or high-profile biennale, bought off the shelf or ordered to a specified size. Prove your non-racist credentials by getting your constituents to pay for the New Statues and daring them to criticise the decision. Price has received puff pieces in *The Guardian* (house journal for the art-commissioning class) thereby making the artist first-choice for anyone lining up a New Statue as a civic-diversity gesture.

If you criticise on grounds of aesthetics you are missing

the point. The appearance of New Statues does not matter. Authorities might as well place in that location a sign that says "average black woman". These are literally tokens on a board, intended to demonstrate not virtues or achievements, but racial, ethnic or religious characteristics, used to demarcate captured areas. This is how the people who place these markers feel. They state it explicitly. New Statues are designed to be boring because they were always intended to be tokens. They have to be absolutely unambiguously a token, as legible and unsophisticated as a flag because they demonstrate power. Any veteran of an art-history course (or John Berger television series) will tell you that public art is always a demonstration of power and wealth. This is not entirely wrong, although Marxists overlook aesthetics, the most essential and exciting part of art. No Marxist can ever tell you why one sculpture is more invigorating or moving than another if the difference is mainly in appearance (as opposed to subject). What Marxists get right is that public art is an assertion of dominance, most acutely regarding symbols set up in civic spaces.

Whether Marxist or not, we can conclude that the rich and powerful are seeking to impose Price's black every-women (and similar pieces) on us. To demonstrate what? That the time of the stale pale male is coming to an end? That bold assertive beautiful Women of Colour™ are the future and you better get used to it? That Italian Renaissance architecture, London parks and Dutch train stations are better for being diversified? The proliferation of New Statues says that you have no choice and no place where you can nurture the illusion that you live in a non-multi-ethnic society. It says questions of appropriacy, tone, scale and mode—let alone aesthetics—that you consider should be addressed are not only irrelevant but simply covert racism. After all, only a racist would object to giant gold statue with the appearance of enlarged plastic figurine placed next to the sanctuary of some of Western culture's most sublime achievements.

The logic of using culture to assert identity—rather than culture embodying (and being come to understood as) an expression of the spirit of the people and artist—is the mechanised stripping down of art. You do not make flags that are subtly painted, include variation, play with form and so on; flags are made to be uniform, legible and unambiguous so that they may be recognised from a distance. Thereafter, flags are symbols, not considered as a unique physical objects. They are made to be not looked at. We register the space of Times Square, New York City (a world-famous location) is now occupied by a symbol of an ethnic minority and we cease to look at the statue. We are aware that a high-value space has been demarcated by those with sufficient money and power as territory under a symbol that indicates the hegemony of ethnic minorities. Ignore the New Statue as we do (indifferent, sympathetic or hostile), we are nevertheless subconsciously aware of how that location is dominated by an assertive political symbol.

The State Art nexus dominates civic spaces through the imposition of endless giant aesthetically inert statues of overweight women slouching and sulking in every square and beside every monument across the land; they can never be removed and you are being dared to oppose these ugly effronteries. You do not object because you know that there is a likelihood of you being smeared as a racist. What is nagging at you (aside from objections regarding scale, placement and appropriacy) is the inkling that what you are seeing is not sculpture or art but territorial capture and occupation.

What is most sobering is not this conclusion that art is a political weapon of control and that this is wrong but that this is inevitable and that were we (or people sympathetic to our ideals) in power, we would be well advised to use art in that way too. The bitterest pill for the aesthete—one who has distained identity politics and sought always a glorious detachment from material-political readings of art—is acknowledging that tokens matter and that our side's tokens should matter more than those of others. That does not preclude having considerations of form and wishing for art to aspire to the ineffable, also wishing to preserve the best of the past in a judicious way. But what it does mean is that we should—that we unavoidably must—use art as an assertion of values in a way that will sometimes be crude and deployed in an instrumentalist fashion.

Even more painful, for an author who wrote an entire book advocating restraint and the preservation of ideologically objectionable art[1], is accepting the reality that many New Statues will have to go. I do not support destruction but the majority of the ideological tokens placed in our public spaces and designed to disfigure and provoke (especially in historical sites or places of great beauty) will have to be removed. You cannot overthrow a regime and keep its flags flying over your castles, halls and government buildings; in fact, you cannot have these flags in any civic spaces, although you could allow people to fly them over private property. Statues standing for the liberalist order will have to be relocated, sold, returned to the artist and so on. Ones with artistic merit in less prominent places might be kept as object lessons or preserved, taking into account the local community's genuine attachment.

When I wrote in my book about people reacting strongly against symbols of a tyrannical regime which had oppressed them, I was thinking of statues of Saddam Hussein and Joseph Stalin. What I had not recognised was the tyranny of liberalism, which destroys communities and traditions,

---

1   Iconoclasm, Identity Politics and the Erasure of History

undermines customs, deliberately deracinates its population, suppresses free speech and association. Suppressive and humiliating control is not a phenomenon distanced by time or continent; it is something we ourselves have lived through. Softness and indirectness of the presentation of liberalism's absolutist position is a protective strategy, as well as advantageous self-deception. Speaking out (without advocating violence or even criminal action) is penalised, with expression of Orwellian "thought crime" punished as hate speech. New Statues are indicative of a liberalist regime that treats as racial bigotry objecting to an incongruous and ugly statue disfiguring a public space. In fact, New Statues are not just signs of such a regime, they are the tools of that regime, deployed as provocation. They are bait used to entrap conservatives, reactionaries and anyone with strong aesthetic objections to inappropriate interventions in civic spaces.

New Statues are tokens used to occupy territory, symbols used to demonstrate the values of the elite and lures to trap opponents of the elite. I take that bait now, willingly, and serve you as a sin-eater—a shunned wanderer in Welsh tradition who consumes a meal at the house of a dead person in return for taking on the burden of the deceased's sins. I am destined to be treated as a pariah for saying things you know to be true but cannot yourself utter.

Price and other sculptors are probably unaware of the utility that the elite find in his figures. It is perhaps fitting that liberalism (the most indirect and self-deceiving of absolutist ideologies) uses material (produced by duped accomplices) of the blandest kind to express its values and to impose its will upon a population numbed by a stream of unstoppable and irreversible counter-traditional actions. As historic skylines are destroyed by rampant skyscraper-building in order for mayors to mark their legacies and property speculators acquire profits, the banal everyman statue is only a slight insult to taste and dignity. The apathy with which New Statues are received shows how beaten down today's population is. Unable to state that the ugly and inappropriate is unwelcome, we have been gagged by the elite that says our society is the most humane and open in history. New Statues are routinely introduced to "start a dialogue", but even the common man now knows this is a trap. He knows that as soon as he speaks honestly he knows he will be called a bigot and subjected to public humiliation. Such feelings of powerlessness and resentment do not easily dissipate. Perhaps not far off is a day when these New Statues will be toppled and defaced as Stalin's effigies were in Budapest or Saddam Hussein's were in Baghdad.

31 May 2025

FOURTEEN

DROWN EVERYTHING

In Bristol July 2020 a mob of left-wingers, anarchists and black race activists were enabled by the mayor to topple a statue of Edward Colston, a great man who made a contribution to the wealth, wellbeing and education of the city's population. For years, activists had been claiming that Colston had benefited from colonial plantations that employed slave labour and had agitated for the removal of the statue and the removal of his name from buildings and streets in the city. Unable to do so through democratic means (local residents had resisted these attempts) the combination of obedience to authority and a sense of exceptionality arising from the COVID lockdown and the hysteria over the death of George Floyd permitted a mob to be set upon the statue.

It was simultaneously a way of enacting ritual humiliation on a symbol of mercantilist philanthropy and an expression of a petulant child's resentment of the authority and achievement of a father whom they know they can never match. Despite their expressed intentions to overcome the past, the rioters were showing the powerful sway of the city forefathers had over them, implicitly acknowledging their greatness. One does not hate the insignificant, only the notable. Iconoclasm is too often thought of in simple terms, as merely a rejection of an order symbolised by physical culture, prompting its defacement or destruction. Iconoclasm can encompass a violent disruption of an object not because the violator rejects the power of the object but precisely because he recognises and fears the power of the object.

When the sites of ancient Egyptian settlement were excavated in the European colonial period, Western archaeologists were puzzled to discover upended carved effigies with watermarks. The marks were not part of the sedimentary formation of the material but a post-carving state. The watermarks revealed that rather than a result of a period of flood while the statues had been in situ, the statues had been prone. In other words the submergence had occurred in conjunction with toppling and seemed to have been deliberate. This presented evidence of deliberate drowning that was present in tombs robbed in ancient times. It was believed that tomb statues were physical receptacles for the spirit of the dead person and were able to observe and perhaps protect the grave. Robbers did not defile or drown statues out of malice or mere exuberant vandalism but in order to preserve themselves from the supernatural power that was channelled through the statue.

The drowning of idols that parallels that of the action of carvers in some ancient cultures, where the tools used to make a sacred sculpture were afterward thrown into a river to ensure they could never be sullied in the production of non-sacred effigies. Water has transformative power for both the carver and the thief. As well as a means of hiding evidence, suffocating the living man and the living supernatural effigy, water is also conduit to the watery underworld, a place of incomprehensible wonders and terrors, home of the supernatural.

In "Art as Attrition" I suggested that it would be perhaps be necessary to remove New Statues. I do not advocate literal drowning or other forms of destruction, even as a response to art that is a extension of the ideology of a hateful regime. While the deliberate action of holding at a distance the ideals instilled by progressivist education will be accompanied by the removal of New Statues that symbolise the liberalist creed, that should done with care and legally, allowing artists and interested parties the chance to purchase the statues.

Enculturation of liberalist standards gives rise to idols that dominate our mental landscape. Liberal idols of the sacred concepts of egalitarianism, equality, democracy, multiculturalism, atomised individualism and materialism have to be drowned if we are to break free of our conditioning and return to a historical norm. This will temporarily take away the power of these idols but do not make the error of thinking this could destroy the idols nor defeat the spirit that erected them. They will always be there, ready to emerge from the water and subject you to their powerful sway. Stay vigilant and keep them submerged—breathless, blinded, hidden—so that they cannot exert their influence over you.

Drown your regret at having wasted your time devoting yourself to lies you were told. Drown the shame you feel about having been so cautious when you could have been bold. Drown the truisms you have heard about the art world—that it is meritocratic, objective, benign, aesthetically responsive, centred around appreciation of a given object. Whatever aspirations you have, keep them separate from your assumptions. Do not confuse the two. The truth is that arts funding may once have been linked to quality but it is no longer and has not been so for some time. The channels that were meant to support art now support artists—essentially client groups who do the bare minimum in order to receive stipends from their political allies in the technocracy. Hence the rise of political-social activism in collective groups. Once your activities have been described as art, you are available to turn cultural funding towards political ends and personal sustenance. It does not matter how good you are, your art is not eligible for support because the criteria have been changed to exclude you. Remember that you are hated, dismissed or completely ignored by the echelons of administrators of civic patronage, ostensibly open to your application submissions.

When I urge to drown your idols, it is done on the understanding that you will never be properly free of their baleful influence. Indeed, it is precisely because complete freedom from that enculturation is not possible that such a mental discipline is recommended. Far from a dismissal of the sacred power of an idol, drowning is an acknowledgement of this force and an attempt to overcome it not through denial but through an act of appropriate deference-defiance. In the same way that a man prone to violence is always aware of his strength and the way an alcoholic knows alcohol has a potency for him that is awful, do not underestimate the hold your education has over you. Drowning is a conscious activity of keeping the drowned object submerged, visible to you but separated by a barrier of protective water—mutable fugitive water that could disappear and allow the idol to breathe again and once again fix you in its grip.

4 June 2025

FIFTEEN

TWELVE RULES FOR ARTISTS

In going where you have to go, and doing what you have to do, and seeing what you have to see, you dull and blunt the instrument you write with. But I would rather have it bent and dull and know I had to put it on the grindstone again and hammer it into shape and put a whetstone to it, and know that I had something to write about, than to have it bright and shining, and nothing to say, or smooth and well-oiled in the closet, but unused.

Ernest Hemingway, 1938

1. Take yourself seriously

If you don't take yourself seriously, no one else will. Not being serious about yourself will give others a reason to dismiss you; people are always in need of reasons not to think. Don't take yourself too seriously but remember you are capable of intelligent insights and admirable action, even if that is infrequent and emerges in an unintended manner. Being open to your capacity for greatness contributes to your awareness of yourself. You are a spiritual being capable of experiencing the transcendent and (through art) assisting others in that. This makes you potentially a conduit for the divine. Artists are types of visionaries, scryers and shamans. Even if you are a trickster who is playful in his art, be aware that your humour is more than flippancy. Humour never need be frivolous because wit springs from the human capacity for lateral thinking and meaningful analogy. Your art is work, never just play; it is never inconsequential. Through play we discover what the world is and what we are.

2. *Find friends*

Find friends. These may be artists, writers and others open to the arts or just people you can talk to and whose company enriches you. It is good if they share your moral, spiritual and political values. Absolute alignment between them and you is unnecessary; you and they will adjust naturally. You do not need to share aesthetic tastes—it benefits you to be in frequent contact with someone whose appreciation and knowledge is different from yours—but you must be able to talk well and honestly about what is exciting. Listen a lot; don't automatically reject; think about their views. True friends will not prevent you from taking risks. Your courage will inspire them to be freer of oppressive orthodoxy. Discussing your advances will sharpen your own insight and understanding into your art and how you came to create it. Friends will support you when you are spurned; they will prick your pomposity when you are acclaimed.

3. *Look at and talk about art seriously*

You need to recognise success and failure and articulate those qualities. Get into the habit of framing what you know in verbal terms, while never forgetting that art operates most (and most importantly) subverbally. Art causes responses that are visceral and instinctual, like a spasm of memory. It cannot be properly put into words but to approach the response in words is worthwhile. Observe closely the means and messages of art. Concentrate on great art; explain some key elements. Don't be embarrassed about the inadequacy of your words; a real and honest response is valuable mental training; your framing doesn't have to be fixed. Apply what you learn from the great and apply it all levels. When dealing with the minor be generous and praise successes, as this makes you grander and more complete in your magnanimity and any lack of pettiness. When you criticise be ready to adjust your view. Debate art like it matters. Don't be afraid of being passionate and assertive but have the grace to consider other views—before you demolish them. Be generous and informed, free of spite and archness. We don't need any more commissars or hollow-headed followers.

4. Work for your people

Your people are your blood kith and kin, your local community and your artist brethren. Commit to their welfare. That commitment may take the form of art making, writing and so forth; it may also come as community action, charity, assisting colleagues, teaching, donating art and so forth. The state is not the people; in the West today, the state is mostly the enemy of the people. Your nation (as distinct from the state) may not appreciate or support your work—this should be a matter of indifference to you—but do not work against the best interests of your nation. Do not work for the state unless in ways that also benefit your people, your colleagues and your values. Do not rely on the state for direct patronage and never rely on it for a livelihood, honours or approval; you may take only from the state only in so far as you never depend on it and never injure your people. Make your people richer, stronger, happier, more united. You have no responsibilities to anyone who is outside your people, although you can undertake other responsibilities when they do not conflict with the wellbeing of your people. Never place your faith in the state.

5. Balance group interest and self-interest

There will be times for difficult decisions. You will have to turn down group events to focus on your own welfare. You will decline invitations to exhibit, publish, serve on a committee or assist a project. Part of this is quality control—don't let yourself or colleagues down by doing substandard work—but partly it is the necessity of preserving autonomy. Generally, I advise you to sign letters of protest and manifestoes, even if you have doubts about the efficacy or content of an action, because generosity in helping your shared cause bonds you and your colleagues; it advances your people overall. Do not fall into the trap of hyper-individualism of liberalism and romanticism, which lauds disdainful isolation. When we are in a struggle of civilisational degradation, atomisation is the surest path to demoralisation and defeat. The free-rider figure of the lone romantic can only be borne by society when it is flourishing, healthy and bountiful. We have long passed that point. If in doubt, commit to group action and solidarity. You will know when it is time to stand back, but you only earn that right to reticence and discrimination once you have served your people and your cause reliably and bravely over a long period.

6. With alacrity make, destroy, monitor

A. Make art often

Most often one regrets what one doesn't do more often than what one does do. So, if you have time and inclination, do. Make what you can. Remember you do not have to share what you make. You can be in private when you undertake experiments. Practice will give you fluency; even routine work can open doors as long as you are attuned to what is before you. Build your stamina so that when really great work demands of you great effort that you are capable of rising to the challenge without flinching.

B. Destroy a lot

It does you good to destroy your work and relinquish the substandard. Reuse your material when you can. Without the ability to be ruthless, you will accumulate too much and will be unable to see your achievements clearly. You will incur costs that will burden you with preserving the poor and thereby prevent you from making the better. Take pride in the best you have done and do not become too sentimental regarding the weak, secondary or superseded. Preserve samples of preparatory materials, experiments and unfinished pieces, but preserve sparingly.

C. Quality matters

You are responsible for what becomes public. Hold yourself to the highest standards. Do not let yourself down or sell your art short by allowing yourself to produce substandard pieces. Once out in the world, poor piece will inform any-one with eyes that you lack competence, conscientiousness or judgment. They will give licence for others even less disciplined than you to slacken control of what is made and made public. Don't discredit yourself and your cause by lacking restraint or seriousness.

7. Keep records

Get into the habit of keeping sketchbooks and notes and preserving them. For your own organisation and the benefit of collectors, dealers and historians, know what you make, record it and take photographs (both after and during the making). Try to give fixed titles and serial numbers to track items. Write notes about what you make. These do not have to be lengthy or definitive; they do not have to reveal sources or subjects. Remember that definitive declarations can repel or distract viewers. Factual information about what was done when, why and what your thoughts were regarding the art may prove of value to yourself and others. Don't let recordkeeping prevent you from selling a picture you haven't documented properly, if it comes to a choice between selling and not selling. Art must (from time to time) take flight and disappear from your corpus.

8. Write letters

Not just email but letters can be written to communicate your work or circumstances. You will think more clearly if you have to explain your activity to a colleague, friend or collector. It will preserve this information in the same way that a notebook or sketchbook would. You don't have to write at too great a length or too deeply; you are an artist not a philosopher or theorist. Letters and cards build connections between you, colleagues and collectors. They force you to operate outside of the visual realm and approach ideas verbally. If you have the inclination, drawings or photographs can be included. Collectors especially value these in relation to piece they have acquired. The creations of ties that bind you, your art and others who appreciate your art are a vital component of making a living network of independent creators and patrons.

9. Art is a social business

Art lives and dies in the care of others. Unless one makes stone grave goods to be unearthed by a later society, one's art passes through the hands of the living. To allow that you must make sure that people want to be with your art and develop an attachment. That can mean telling people about your pictures so they have an entry point—a handle with which they can access your art. It may be that you talk about the motivation to make the image or a group of works by other artists which are comparable to what you have done. This will require communication in person through letters or conversation and by social media, blogging or journalising. It can mean (distasteful as it may be to your temperament) making people care about you, not in the sense of eliciting charity through pity, but getting others to buy into your earnestness and unique qualities as an artist and them wanting to own a part of that story and assist you in the journey. Sometimes it is the vanity of wishing to acquire the prestige of being enlightened and bold enough to support an artist on their way to glory. However it is got, that personal connection to art and artist is what—before any monetary considerations come into it—delivers your art into the hands of someone who will care for it.

10. Find homes for your art

Your art is well served by finding a good home. If you cannot find a home, make one by cultivating someone who cares about you and your art but otherwise wouldn't consider owning original art usual for them. You may have to sell art to someone who wants decoration, a gift, to show off or offer you a helping hand. The person may consider your art a marker of social status. If you can avoid such transactions do, even if it negatively affects your situation or standing, because always submitting to necessity makes you indebted and submissive. This attitude has a way of creeping into other aspects of your life and compromising you. A habit can become a mindset, which can blot out the more noble qualities, which wither. All except the fortunate rich have to strive to succeed but your dignity counts for much. As soon as you can, refuse offers that demean you or diminish your art. These opportunities should go to artists younger and poorer than you. If your art is worthy of attention, it is worthy of the sentimental attachment of a loving owner. Lay the groundwork to allow your art to flourish without you.

11. *Take risks*

If you are going to embrace your destiny and fulfil your potential you must take risks. Being too cautious will kill your art (and spirit) more surely than an error of judgment or a failed gamble. Many buccaneers wagered their fortunes and lost them, knowing that they could earn back the riches they had lost. To explore your capacity you must make art that appears strange or ugly. There is nothing sadder than the sight of an artist too timid to set foot outside his house, anxiously eyeing the clouds above. Don't be frightened of life or of your darker aspects; that darkness can be the horse to which you can hitch your chariot or plough. There may be elements of your self that provoke disquiet and shame; they can never be curbed until you can look unflinchingly at them, sometimes through the lens of your art. The risks are not primarily stylistic or technical but the fortitude in confronting internal conflict. To do this you will have take a stance independent of your colleagues, which may incur hostility and incomprehension. Let neither friends nor foes dictate what excites you, animates you and what you may say. You must test your discretion about when to be brave but there will come a time when you must be brave or you will cease to be. Extinction of the self comes about through failure of will and nerve. No one expects perfect judgment but they expect you to show your mettle.

12. *Take responsibility, suffer well*

To be an artist at the highest level is to take on the responsibility of a seer, thinker, leader, pathfinder, truthteller. It is a position of moral and metaphysical trust. You must be true to your cause, your people, your role. This takes strength, courage, care and patience. If you break new ground people will resent it and mischaracterise your efforts; you may be scorned and rejected. These are incidental—pay them no mind. Do not allow suffering to be the centre of your life. Accept your rejection but do not court it or fetishise it. You have been chosen by fate to serve your people and (indirectly) humanity at large in a way that will be appreciated by few. Isolation is inevitable and irrelevant. Accept suffering required without complaint and self-pity, both of which would distract you and assault your dignity. Even, at the highest level, greatness is irrelevant. Man is not made for himself alone. You were made to serve your art and your people. Action and thought count. To do wonderful things means to suffer. Make greatly. Suffer well.

8 June 2025

SIXTEEN

LETTERS

These letters and postcards (whole and in extract) address questions of bravery, risk-taking, overcoming barriers and broader issues, such as the motivation to make art and how art is received. Readers are suggested to consult the chronology at the end of this volume, as that will explain the author's location and circumstances when the correspondence was written.

Observations in the correspondence have a scattered quality. Should you prefer more measured thinking, it can be found in my monographs, articles and reviews. You may find these letters lacking substance, reasoning and sophisticated argumentation. (I have been told I do not have any gift for abstract thinking and that may be so.) Any value in these excerpts lies in epigrammatic pithiness, strength of expression and freewheeling quality—ideas worked out in rough as they arise, clumsily, doubtingly and without recourse to reference materials. These letters weave in observations and recommendations that appear in my essays and books, showing how ideas emerge through practice, what some call the process of praxis. I am not sure I would claim anything as sophisticated as that for these extracts but they do illuminate how I have attempted (and sometimes failed) to apply ideals in my own activities.

The texts were not written for publication and that shows in their deficits. I do not know how artists of other eras and places talk to each other but this is how the artists in my circle express themselves. I do not believe art—at least, the sort of art that is serious and is of lasting consequence—is primarily an intellectu-

al activity. Making art can involve the intellect but what really counts is the visual appeal, emotional engagement and memorability of visual art. Definitions here are loose. "Post-Modernism" (for example) is used as shorthand for an approach or attitude to art rather than an approximation of concepts originated by Derrida, Baudrillard and others. The artists I know do not devour theoretical texts nor have much respect for artists who labour over complicated intellectual frameworks. These letters ultimately derive from the way I talked as a student at Goldsmiths in the 1990s. Not all students or tutors there conversed in such a way; indeed, the abrupt, dismissive and emphatic style of speaking and writing came about among some of us as a way of pricking the pretensions of conceptual and political opponents within the art world (including the convenor groups and tutorials of our college).

Notes have been added for lesser known artists and events of particular relevance. Recipients of correspondence are named when they are public figures and identified by initials when they are less well-known or have indicated that they prefer to have their identities concealed. It is often the case today that artists and writers cannot reveal their true thoughts on subjects due to social mores or political consequences; they cannot even associate with controversial figures. It is my hope that this book might make more people braver about dissenting; without bravery not only does our civilisation collectively fall but we all individually fall.

[letter to LGM]

Berlin, 19.VII.2009

Dear L.

I have had a few models, though generally I work from photographs. [...] Often one works from the photographic source and reconceptualises the form into an imagined entity in three dimensions. This is useful when a passage in the source is ambiguous or unsatisfying. One uses one's memory and skill to picture the figure in space and find a way of conveying that understanding by altering the painting—that is, making the painting deviate from a literal transcription. The distortions make the image more legible or tangible or realistic or uglier/more comely. The source is only ever a source. The painted image must work in its own terms. When adhering to the source damages my intentions I will alter the image from the source without compunction. Sometimes the photographic illegibility or oddness has potency, so it is retained in the painting. There are no firm rules. Art is in the application of skill and judgement.

So, working from a model is a totally different experience to using photographs. The outcome from life drawing/painting is usually not a consideration for me. It is the training and insight it gives me into the human form and into working practice and application of skill that overrides the desire to "make a picture". Whether I end up with a good, bad or indifferent picture (or even no finished picture at all) is beside the point.

[extract of letter to S.]

Berlin, 9.VIII.2009

Dear S.

I have just finished three small gouaches of a woman bathing. One will be part of the set submitted for the London exhibition this winter.[1] The original source is a photograph of a woman washing in a shallow tub, in the manner of Degas's figures. She crouches with her back to the viewer, light falling through an open window above her in the background. My paintings haven't done the original justice. Conceptually the painting is pretty tight but that's never enough. Another pair of paintings is of two standing nudes, again backs to the viewer. [...] I am developing a group from which a set of four can be selected for London.

---

1   Probably "The Discerning Eye", Mall Galleries, London, 12-22 November 2009.

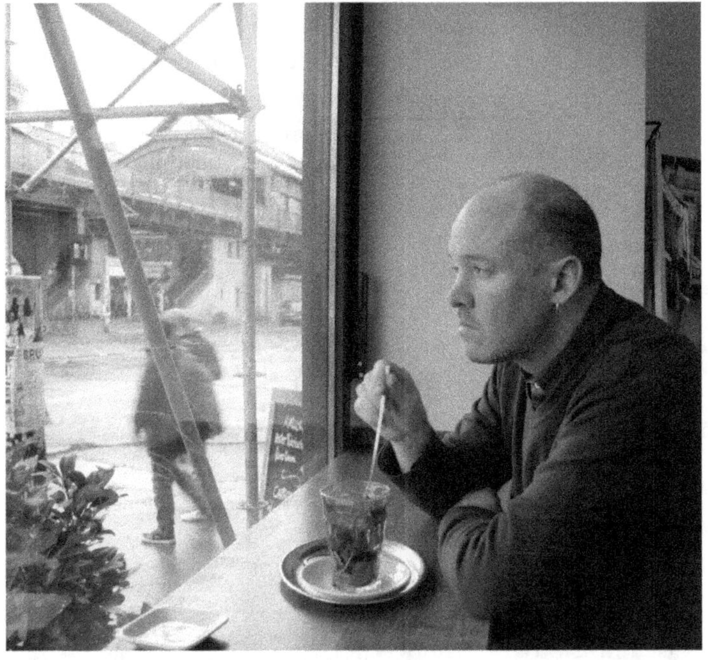

AA at Café Manolo, Eberswalder Kreuzung, Berlin, 19 February 2013

[postcard of Degas's Après le bain, femme s'essuyant la nuque to LGM]

Berlin, 12.X.2009

Dear L.

I'm sitting in Manolo, my favourite café, watching the busy Eberswalder Kreuzung[2]: cars and pedestrians in the driving rain. (I leave the flat when the cleaner is there.) Degas is one of the best artists for capturing the nude. He was exceptionally clever. Do you see the way the marks describing

2   German: Eberswalder (Strasse) crossroads, in Prenzlauer Berg

the figure don't follow the direction of the limbs or the lengths of the muscles? Instead they are primarily vertical. Half close your eyes and the form becomes solid and you see the sheen on the skin. That is one of the tests for a successful picture. Maybe one day I could make something similar—that would be a great achievement.

Take care

A.

[postcard of Delvaux's L'éloge de la Melancholie to Simon Wilson[3]]

St Idesbald, Belgium, 14.X.2010

After inhabiting Delvaux's world for 20 years I finally arrive here.[4] A tremendous collection & moving experience. Town almost too picturesque—some views familiar from PD's paintings. Seeing the early work made me think he was ambitious & competent from early (*Grand nu rose* (1929)). Heard head curator approached Tate a decade ago re solo show and was rebuffed. Time for a big British retrospective!

Regards

A.

3   British art historian and author Simon Wilson OBE (b. 1942) was a senior administrator at the Tate Gallery 1967 to 2002. His interests in erotic art, Surrealism, Schiele, Dalí and other topics overlap with Adams's. Wilson was an early supporter of Adams's art and writing.
4   Belgian Surrealist painter Paul Delvaux (1897-1994) was greatly admired by Adams, who wrote about him often. Delvaux's house-museum is located on the Flanders coast at St Idesbald.

[postcard of Wiertz's La Belle Rosine to David Lee[5]]

Bruxelles, 16.X.2010

Extremely impressed by Musée Wiertz.[6] I can easily manage 1,000 words on him. Rather a complex & contradictory artist—more than the purveyor of grand guignol, he was also a social reformer & a generous man. He painted plenty of bad pictures but more than a few good ones. The largest canvases are truly vast. He also invented a new (and ineffective) technique of essence on unprimed linen. Meunier[7] can be summarised in a few paragraphs.

Regards

AA

[postcard of Delvaux's studio to Basil Beattie[8]]

Bruxelles, 17.X.2010

Reviewing Delvaux (exhib. + museum) and Wiertz. Also delivering gouaches to my gallerist here. Saw an Ensor show here. The best paintings are unbelievable—breathtaking. Such fluency, boldness and acuteness! *Intrigue* is perfect.[9]

---

5   British art critic David Lee (b. 1953) was (from 2000) founder-editor of *The Jackdaw* newsletter, for which Adams started to write in 2004.

6   Belgian Antoine Wiertz (1806-1865) was a Romantic-Symbolist painter, whose museum is in the centre of Brussels. Adams published articles mentioning him multiple times.

7   Belgian sculptor Constantin Meunier (1831-1905), whose museum is in Brussels.

8   British painter Basil Beattie RA (b. 1935) was a tutor at Goldsmiths College during Adams's time there. Although not assigned to him as a student, Adams elected to consult Beattie often during 1994-5.

9   Belgian Symbolist James Ensor (1860-1949) painted *Intrigue*

The facture and colour [are] rich but not self-indulgent—masterful! Will write 5 reviews in the coming week. Then I have 4 small canvases to paint for a show here (Nov.). Hope your own art is coming on well.

   Regards

AA

[postcard of Vermeer's Woman Reading a Letter at a Window to Donald Lee[10]]

Dresden, 10.IX.2010

In Dresden to review Vermeer[11] for *The Jackdaw*[12] (Nov.). Did you see my "Menzel" in Sep. issue? I keep noticing faults in Rembrandt & still don't warm to Rubens. Do you think I'm ill, perhaps? Surprised by an affecting self-portrait aged 20 by pastelliste Theresa Concordia Maron (1725-1806). Do you know of her? She is new to me but it is not my area. Vermeer show small but at least I could *see* it (no crush). *Masson* & *Beckmann* should be published soon.

   Grüßen aus Dresden![13]

AA

(1890), an oil painting in the collection of the Royal Fine Art Museums of Belgium.

10   Literary editor of *The Art Newspaper*, for which Adams reviewed.

11   "Der frühe Vermeer (The Young Vermeer)", Gemäldegalerie Alte Meister, Dresden, 3 September-28 December 2010.

12   *The Jackdaw*, founded by David Lee in 2000, is an independent art newsletter. Adams first wrote for it in 2003 and from 2007 onwards contributed to every issue.

13   German: Greetings from Dresden.

[postcard of Manet's Lunch in the Studio (detail) to TT]

Berlin, 21.III.2011

I went to the vernissage in Neukölln to support my model FK, who danced there. The dance was the best thing there. The art was Not Very Good—but I find most art Not Very Good. I left as soon as the dance finished. Here is a part of a Manet painting demonstrating his technique of energy, brevity and accuracy. He forgets his marks & forgets himself and expresses his subject alone. There is a charming & vigorous painting of a house by Manet in the Alte Nationalgalerie—I am sure you know it. Next time you visit look again.

Best wishes

A.

[postcard of Gravelines to TT]

Gravelines, 13.IV.2011

Paying homage to Seurat, who painted here. The light is striking. I made a few sketches but will leave tomorrow. Would like to return. The museum of drawing[14] is in an old fort on the coast. The gallery is inside the fortifications. I shall visit tomorrow & interview the director. [...]

A.

[postcard of Magritte's La Magie Noire to Simon Wilson]

Ghent, 14.IV.2011

It should be Van Eyck not Magritte but I only just arrived, fresh from Gravelines. Considering an article on Marcel

14   Actually the museum of printmaking.

Gromaire[15], whose etchings I saw in Gravelines. Saw where Seurat painted in Gravelines. Viewed Rops[16] sketches & albums with his drawings & photos. His *Eros Crucified* pastel was in a store room, framed under a custom-made case. Handled Delvaux's sketchbooks. (Both in [the Royal Library,] Bruxelles.) Seem to have enough material for articles. Will see Rouault tomorrow. Then back to Bruxelles to deliver 2 oils to Émilie.[17] [...]

Regards

AA

[postcard of Schiele's Sitzendes Mädchen to EJ]

London, 29.VI.2011

Never be ashamed of loving great artists, no matter how popular they are, E----! The Schiele drawing show in London is *astonishing*.[18] He is one of the greatest draughtsman of all time. The lines are firm & bold, the compositions exciting and colouring v. powerful—esp. because it is so sparing. Lovely restrained portraits as well as sexually supercharged nudes. I'll show you the catalogue when I return. Also a show of [Louise] Bourgeois prints—disappointingly unmemorable, a little lazy and careless. I spent almost £100 on sketchbooks—my only addiction. Do you have addictions? Hope you are drawing & all is well.

Regards

---

15   French painter-printmaker Marcel Gromaire (1892-1971), known for his Social Realist art.
16   Belgian artist Félicien Rops (1833-1898), known for his erotic art. Adams visited Rops's museum in Namur.
17   French gallerist Émilie Dujat, whose Galerie Libertine, Brussels exhibited Adams's art.
18   "Egon Schiele: Women", Richard Nagy Gallery, London, 19 May-30 June 2011.

Alexander

[postcard of Adams's Congress to SW]

Berlin, 1.VIII.2011

I'll be flying into JFK on 22 Sept. & will be in NYC & WDC until 4 Oct., when my residency commences. Thereafter I'll be in [Connecticut] until 30 Nov.; 30 Nov.-7 Dec. I'll be in NYC again before flying to the UK. Hope I'll be able to catch up with you & Ian at least once during that time. Haven't seen Carolyn recently but should see her this week. Looking forward to the Degas show in Boston & de Kooning in NYC (MoMA) (& Picasso at the Frick). All ok here except I am terribly broke. [Exhibition in] LA sold well for me but only small paintings at low prices, otherwise dead. Do you know any collectors? I'll bring small b&w paintings with me in Sept. Any connections welcome.

    See you soon?

A.

[letter to Roger Bates[19]]

Paris, 11.II.2012

Dear Roger

A few notes from my time here. Apologies in advance for the random assortment of observations. Arrived yesterday early enough to visit Musée Rodin on Boulevard des Invalides. Unfortunately, the main part of museum (incl. Hôtel Brion) is closed for refurbishment (bane of off-season visitors). The current exhibition is of drawings. Curious

---

19   British artist Roger Bates (1947-2021) was the course leader for the BA Fine Art/History of Art degree course at Goldsmiths College while Adams was a student.

things. I'm collecting my thoughts, which will appear as "Lost in Paris" in *Jackdaw*'s May edition. I'm not sure if he's a good draughtsman—inventive, prolific, daring, sometimes effective? Definitely! But "good"? Not certain. Maybe I won't reach a conclusion. Afterwards made a short tour of the garden—very elegant, French-style formal garden, conical firs & straight paths. (One can see that at Sanssouci in Potsdam.) Figures bundled against the cold, posing for snapshots next to bronze nudes. (Thoughts of icy weather & brass monkeys.)

Today Musée Bourdelle. Didn't know much of Bourdelle[20] other than *The Archer Herakles*, *Les Pommes* and the fact he was Giacometti's master. Expected his museum to be small, domestic, dusty and neglected (à la Meunier's). Yet when I arrived it was modern (in part), well staffed and attended and *very* big. The main hall has original plasters, many monumental, and side galleries have maquettes, coloured plasters, busts. Then further galleries had a large display of *his* drawings then a large basement area had more bronzes. All this plus his original apartment, studio (closed when I went), Carrière's studio[21], an upstairs terrace and two gardens (small, with large bronzes). It was bitingly cold but even so I could tell it must be charming on a warm evening. The reliefs are a bit like [Eric] Gill's. A beautiful head like a Pre-Raphaelite belle, all sharp nose, wide cheekbones and full lips. A bit Rodin (his master). Wish there had been more like that but commissions paid his wages and these pieces are a bit grand & dull. Even so, he's not the dry old stick I imagined him to be.

Then the Louvre. Well, you know how huge it is; beyond

20   French sculptor Antoine Bourdelle (1861-1929), whose museum is at 18 rue Antoine Bourdelle, Paris.
21   French artist Eugène Carrière (1849-1906), whose studio-museum is adjacent to Bourdelle's.

the scope of a letter. I was decidedly glad Salles 63-75 were closed for rehanging. Salle 6 was a miserable place, hordes pressing forward to photograph *La Gioconde*. La Grande Galerie is as busy and noisy as a railway station platform. Had a look at Mantegna's *Crucifixion*. Complicated, in a perspectival sense. It has held its colour well compared to the *St Sebastian*, which is reduced to almost grisaille. Looked at Raphael a little. What a repulsive picture Leonardo's *St John* is! The pneumatic flesh, the smirk, the inarticulated hand. Mind you, I was sorry not to get a ticket to the Leonardo show in London. Chardin—my first real attempt to get to grips with him. Guardi, Titian (so hard to see in Salle 6), *La Belle Jardiniere*, Egyptian heads, Assyrian reliefs, a Messerschmidt head, Poussin (*Self-Portrait, Diogenes Discarding his Bowl*, the landscape of *Orpheus & Eurydice*, the *Four Seasons*), even some Impressionists upstairs (nothing compared to what I saw in America, besides, I am girding myself for Musée d'Orsay tomorrow), and so on. The highlight was the *Avignon Pietà*—as near [as] to perfect an expression of feeling in art as I know. I don't know why, but the early painters got Pietàs more realistic than other paintings of the Passion there is a fine Pietà (by Ercole di Roberti?) in the Walker Art Gallery with similar qualities of close observation and accuracy, as well as a slightly archaic hieratical atmosphere. You sometimes come across that in Early Renaissance wood carvings (German/North European, C15th). Konrad Witz was a painter and a carver, though no one's been able to ascribe any sculpture to him.

Too tired to write more. À demain![22]

12.II.2012

Should mention *Le Radeau de la «Méduse»* (or the wreck thereof). A great painting. Géricault, with his meticulous

---

22   French: Until tomorrow!

preparation, overlooked something: his survivors are far too beefy to have been adrift so long & been so close to starvation.

This morning to Musée d'Orsay. The refurbishment & rehang is an improvement—though my recollection of the former set-up is imprecise. Manet & Cézanne (early) are together; Van Gogh, Gauguin & Bernard are together. A lot of Maillol[23] in the sculpture terrace. Strindberg landscapes (stormscapes?), Redon awful, Moreau disappointing. Moreau treats figures as profiles, counters, he's not engaged by the figure. The compositions have little depth or inter-action between figure, foreground & background: so not even the composition has reality; it doesn't explore a place with potential reality. A beautiful little Bonnard of a mir-ror over a table & shelf, a female torso where the artist's re-flection should have been. So beautifully crafted! Delicate, full of life and light and changeability, the composition so artful but the handling suggesting artlessness—groping, even. When I see a great Bonnard painting it reminds me all over again why I love his art. His work obsesses me more than Degas's and Ingres's because I understand them but never get to the bottom of Bonnard; his well is bottomless.

Saw Gallen-Kallela's exhibition (Finnish realist, later a Symbolist).[24] Early *academies* competent, distinctive North-ern light, but unremarkable. Some fine early portraits and a few very striking peasant scenes. The snowscapes are ap-pealing but his colour on the crude side, drawing perhaps overemphatic. Then he turns to Symbolism, national myths and so on and almost completely loses it—all fineness and observation go, colour becomes cruder. The paintings from

23   French-Catalan Modernist sculptor Aristide Maillol (1861-1944) is noted for his nudes. His museum is at 59-61 rue de Grenelle, Paris.
24   7 February-6 May 2012.

African safaris are terrible—the colour painfully direct, brushwork showy, scenes touristic clichés. A great shame because he had the makings of a fine Scandinavian realist—along the lines of some Swedish painter whose name escapes me (a good example in Ghent). Hmmm, not very helpful for you. Salomon?[25]

The Parisians are not very organised when it comes to press tickets. Both Musée d'Orsay and Musée Maillol hadn't co-ordinated my contact with attachés de presse with front-of-house staff. I was reduced to my pidgin French and presenting my passport. Glad I got into MM that way as the queue to enter was out to Bld Raspail, all because it was the last day of the Pompeii exhibition.[26] Some very elegant kitchenware and a tripod with hinged legs and a handle set into one leg, making it easy to transport when closed. The painting doesn't excite me but some of the sculpture is captivating, especially a bronze youth bearing a tray for wine.

Which leads nicely into Maillol. Great sculptures (almost all bronzes) and surprisingly efficient paintings—the best of his models, nude—imagine Renoir's *Grandes Baigneuses* in more earthy colours and you have the measure of them. The large pastel nudes are v. volumetric—real sculptor's drawings or what one supposes sculptor's drawings to be. Incidentally, rue de Grenoble, where the museum is, has some great architecture. I wish I had time to stop and sketch.

Then to Église de Saint Sulpice, as it is not far from M'dO and MM and I remembered Delacroix had painted murals there. The church is very large—not attractive but imposing. The Delacroix murals are quite intelligent solutions to the restrictions of the space (two facing walls with

25   Danish-Swedish realist painter Geskel Saloman (1821–1902).
26   "Pompéi – un art de vivre", 21 September 2011-12 February 2012.

arched tops, close together). What one doesn't realise from reproductions is how low the viewpoints are and how poor the light. The light was very low when I arrived (and got worse) but Delacroix designed them so the basic forms are comprehensible in half-light. No, I still think his drawing lousy and he's only the fraction of Géricault but *La Mort du Sardanapule*, *Dante's Barque* and the St Sulpice murals are strong paintings. I plan to return to Paris and write another article on the Musées Delacroix and Moreau.

I drew a Baroque sculpture of the *Virgin & Child* in the apse of the church. Quite a *mise en scene*: Virgin standing on a cloud and treading on a serpent, a rounded niche behind with rays of light, the cloud actually emerging and projecting in front of the column framing the scene. The chair was over one of the few heating vents, meaning I could linger. Then down Quai Voltaire—passing Sennelier's shop—where the pavements were encrusted with salt like nacre on a corpse and the crippled women in black hobbled along the Seine soliciting alms.

Cordialement[27]

A.

[letter to Simon Wilson]

Berlin, 25.XI.2012

Dear Simon

Just back from Bruxelles and Paris. Saw a superb exhibition of Soutine at Musée de l'Orangerie.[28] I perused the catalogue afterwards and saw the last solo show of Soutine in Britain was 1963. There's never been one in Berlin. I mentioned that to the Jewish Museum here, so perhaps

27   French: Cordially.
28   "Soutine, l'ordre du chaos", 3 October 2012-21 January 2013.

that will plant a seed. The show made me wish I had a full colourbox and a few dozen canvases but never mind. I was especially impressed by the still-lifes—not just the beef carcases but all of them—the rabbits, fowl, fruit and so forth. I found the gladioli a little dispersed and lacking a satisfying complex structure to grip me. It struck me that my antipathy to "Expressionism" is actually antipathy towards *German* Expressionism, which is the art dictionary illustration for the entry on Expressionism. I respect and admire Schiele and early Kokoschka and Gerstl both painted some fine pictures; likewise Munch, Rouault, Beckmann and the Belgians. In fact, I can see valuable qualities in almost all the Expressionists with the exception of the Germans (Beckmann excused). I loathe the egotism of German Expressionists—their arrogance about imposing themselves on their subjects, their insensitivity, their bloodyminded stubbornness, their half-baked philosophy, their foul palettes, their hysteria. Soutine typifies Expressionist art and he has none of those faults. He's a damn fine painter and I only got that when I saw a lot of his work together in the flesh—on Monday in Paris. There's none to see in Berlin or Britain.

Paris was more tolerable than previously. I spent time with a Parisian friend and she showed me around her quartier. I am engineering a chance to review Dalí at Centre Pompidou.[29] I doubt it will be for *Jackdaw*, as they had a piece on the same artist not long ago. It gives me an excuse to use my Bruxelles room, as I can catch the train from there to Paris. Visited Sennelier and bought a sketchbook. Quai Voltaire is lousy with gypsies turning con tricks. I got caught out the first time. If you were a gullible type you'd believe the pavements there were sprouting gold rings.

More book reviews will include a seven-volume cata-

29   See note 72.

logue raisonné of Rembrandt's etchings. I've also got the gig of reviewing the [Francis] Bacon catalogue raisonné, which I probably told you. Both for *Art Newspaper*.

No other news.

Yrs

A.

[letter to Roger Bates]

Berlin, 2.XII.2012

Dear Roger

Winter has arrived here as it has in England. Light dustings of snow lie on the cars outside. I was walking in Wiener Straße with a friend and the bar lights were illuminating the falling flecks and people on the street huddled against the cold, smoking and drinking beer from bottles. It was a typical berlinerisch scene.

Soon enough I'll be off to Bruxelles and Paris. I will review "Dalí" for *Apollo*. I doubt the curators will be able to resuscitate his late period. 1936 is pretty much the point he stopped making good work and the work before then from 1932 or so had been patchy. Imagine being washed up by the time you are thirty. It was in his psychological make up to fail, to give in to his childish tendencies when surrounded by the docile and compliant. Those years 1929 to 1932 were a period of grace before half a century of rot and bluster. Having seen how he sold out himself, I feel like [one] cannot be too critical of him. I would say he whored himself out but a prostitute is a prostitute and there's some dignity in the honesty. Dalí became an utter fraud. What did for him was not America but Italy—when he thought he was Leonardo's heir and started those Leonardine cavaliers—it gave him an excuse to dash stuff off without caring or trying. He took up an entirely alien vocabulary—the antithesis of the dry, patient Spanish style of Zurbaran and memories from his childhood—and with insincere language and imagery he compromised what was best about his art. From then onwards he was picking up an dropping fads, styles, imagery, terminology and so on as if he was a child rummaging in the dressing-up box. He *was* doing [it] earlier. In that sense he is the quintessential Post-Modernist—in the worst possible way.

This language of contemporary critical theory is shot through with dishonesty and double-think. So many times I sat through group tutorials and listened to students say what they were painting or drawing was a reflection on art's capacity for self-generated critical awareness and whatever and I didn't have the honesty or courage to call them out on their posturing. How can any person believe such statements or—in the event they do believe them—how can they feel such a minute and arid activity worthy of a minute of someone else's time? The fact that generations of students leave art school thinking in these ways is folly. [...] It is a lie, this belief that art resides in ideas and stances, and it is a lie which kills hope and pleasure and honest discussion. I've seen it kill good artists.

Part of the reason I didn't make more of a point of objecting to some of the absurdities served us by tutors was the fact I was still tasting it and deciding whether or not I could stomach the stuff. Then in the autumn of 1994 I knew the stuff was wrong for me at least, even if it wasn't necessarily without foundation. Also it wasn't my business to interrogate (and possibly humiliate) students or even tutors. I won't do it now but I feel I should write a little on the subject and allow people to consider my reasoning. If it helps one or two students to clear their heads and return to their core interests and desires then it will be worth my effort. More and more I feel that those impulses we had when we were young are intuitively correct. We really can love pleasure, horror, to be entranced, beguiled, amused, fascinated, etc. There's no harm in wishing to investigate those feelings or sensations and reproduce them in one's own art. For sure, we grow in sophistication and understanding and taste as we age, but that does not contradict the genuine hold those basic sensations have upon our imagination. So I don't say that we should preserve our attitudes in aspic but we should not be ashamed of them. We should harness them to an adult sensibility to direct our attitude towards art. Think how much happier students and gallery goers would be. There would be a lot of bad art but there's plenty enough of that already.

I was thinking to formulate in terms of a "new salon", having read a book on salon art yesterday. I don't think in terms of opposites or dialectic but I can't see any way of proposing a more fertile and honest language in art criticism and education than by first attacking the dishonesty of the prevailing standard. I suppose it will be chalked up as *Jackdaw* revanchism and win more enemies than friends but it seems evermore evasive of me *not* to address this topic. It has to be right before I publish and there [are] a number of points that are unclear—exactly how one can explain the inclusivity of this new salon while still ascribing to the authorities exclusive and excluding qualities? If one cannot be specific enough about the exact definition of the "new salon", it will just be a gibe at institutions the author is critical of. I've always been very careful to make sure every sentence I publish is factually accurate and justifiable through evidence and logical reasoning. That isn't going to change.

Do you think there is any point in working up these ideas into an article? Is it credible? I don't want to clutter up another reviews in the manner I did with "Kitaj" debating general points.

Thoughts & news welcome.
Regards

A.

[letter to Roger Bates]

Berlin, 6. XII.2012

Dear Roger

Something in particular caught my eye in your new letter. Of Kitaj you write "His graphic felicities and intellectual postures could not withstand a blast of authentic modernism from Caro & co."[30] From this I see you follow the usual line that Modernism is largely defined by plastic qualities, that Greenbergian view that from the Impressionists through the Cubists and so [on] that Modernism resides in (and is largely defined by) its plastic qualities, the drive to purify the medium and so on. Yet you could say that Kitaj follows the line of Modernism that derives from Symbolism and uses juxtaposition to assert the extra-pictorial content has primacy over formal qualities. Surely there are two Modernisms, plastic and symbolic, and K. falls in the latter, with Eliot, Balthus, et al. To be sure, the latter has often been a refuge for closet (and almost outright) conservatives and milquetoast Modrenists [*sic*][31], but isn't it also a legitimate strand? I hasten to add that I think Caro is more committed to Modrenism [*sic*] and that Kitaj was slightly hedging his bets by keeping a foot in both traditionalist and avant-garde camps. I don't find K. insincere but lacking conviction and courage in his artistic outlook. Perhaps I'm being too exacting. Sometimes being very good and

30   British abstract sculptor Anthony Caro (1924-2013) was Bates's tutor at St Martin's College in the 1960s.
31   Typographical errors repeated throughout the letter.

making pleasing art is enough.

Not strictly speaking two books on [Anya] Gallaccio. There is a monograph that will be published this month (which I haven't seen) and a survey of a handful of YBAs (in a book I have received but haven't looked at). I find I can't read a book or view an exhibition and review it some time later. I need to leave looking at books until I am ready to review. I don't always follow my initial reaction but I find I need to have that reaction fresh in my mind when I write. Will send a précis or even a copy of the review when I write it (late January).

First heavy snow today, lying thickly on the bars, streets and trees. Trust the runway of Schönefeld airport will be clear by Saturday in time for my flight to Bruxelles. Then I'm in Paris for "Dalí"[32], then in Berlin for a few days and off to Wales for Xmas and New Year. For once, I feel I've earned a break, though I've had to do nothing this year I didn't enjoy at some level. Let's hope next year is more productive in terms of art.

No Xmas card this year—too chaotic. Apologies.

Modrenist regrads [*sic*]

A.

[extract of letter to Roger Bates]

Berlin, 7.IX.2014

Returned from a day in Hamburg—not even a day. It has a different atmosphere to Berlin. There's barely a pre-War building standing, as you'd expect in that port city. The men wear forage caps and fluorescent trainers. I tried not to look at the women. The Beckmann show[33] was good

---

32   Centre Pompidou, Paris, 21 November 2012-25 March 2013.
33   "Max Beckmann: The Still Lifes", Kunsthalle, Hamburg, 5 September 5 2014-18 January 2015.

and I suspect my review might turn out harsh because I felt his faults were so obvious and correctable despite his achievements. The review is in the form of an argument you have with a colleague whom you admire and respect but disagree with. Is that a fair approach? Should I have been a little more forgiving and accepting? Well, I suppose lovers of Beckmann will already have their minds made up.

The [Caspar David] Friedrichs were wonderful, including *The Wreck of the Hope*. The Böcklin is very effective, with brushed-in blue for the smoke. There was a gloomy and atmospheric Courbet—a coastal cave—just gives me the chills to think of being trapped in such a place. There was little recent art, which was a relief. I decided to give new art a miss, by and large. I enjoy certain artists but I don't want to see such rubbish filling up museum walls where my stuff should be. I hope that when the National Museum of Wales hangs my oil, they'll put it with the Sutherlands, Bacons and Picassos and not the recent art but for purely chronological tidiness I suppose it will go alongside the tat.[34] But they do have an Auerbach. Did you know Tate will hold an Auerbach retrospective next autumn? Can't wait! Looking forward to seeing and reviewing that.

[extract of letter to Brian Sewell[35]]

Cardiff, 8.XI.2014

I find I have ever less interest in contemporary art. There are a handful of abstract painters, Glenn Brown[36] and Ber-

---

34   Adams's painting Boy (version C) had been agreed as a purchase by the National Museum of Wales. It was acquired in 2015.
35   British art critic Brian Sewell (1931-2015) exchanged letters with Adams in the last years of his life.
36   British painter Glenn Brown (b. 1966), studied at Goldsmiths College 1990-2. Articles on him by Adams date from 2009 onwards.

linde de Bruyckere[37] and no else. No one benefits from me pretending to be engaged by poor art. I look ever more at Renoir, Soutine, Bonnard and Munch. I was thrilled by the Schiele exhibition in London—and sorry to miss the New York display. I saw the Rembrandt show[38]—well, the top half of it. The crowding was terrible. I saw glimpses of some great pieces but couldn't bear the miasma. The experience left me rather unhappy, particularly as the art was so good. Rembrandt is great technically not because he invents anything new nor does anything especially difficult (in terms of skill) but because his judgment is so acute that he knows exactly the right times and places to make his touches and to improvise. Perhaps that is one aspect that separates the great artist from the very good. "Sprezzatura" is a word I should use. Rembrandt is also distinguished by his humanity and his range. The comparison between Rembrandt and Shakespeare is a cliché but it is accurate. I really warmed to Rembrandt only in the last years. I always admired his technique and range but I didn't appreciate the humanity and insight until lately. I still think he is a weak colourist, certainly weaker than Giorgione, Titian and some later painters. He had the brain and eye of a draughtsman but the palette of a cook: oxtail, minestrone, brown bean...

37   Belgian sculptor Berlinde de Bruyckere (b. 1964), subject of a number of reviews by Adams.
38   "Rembrandt: The Late Works", National Gallery, London, 15 October 2014-18 January 2015.

[postcard of Berlinde de Bruyckere's studio to Edward Lucie-Smith[39]]

Ghent, 11.XII.2014

Remarkable show here. [Berlinde de Bruyckere] is a wonderful artist—better than [Louise] Bourgeois, I venture. Best figure sculptor [since] Giacometti? My only reservation is the emotional range—an absence of joy & pleasure (which Bacon had, along with the suffering). Withal she is a wonderful depicter of flesh & meat, wax as fat, wood as bone. Will write review & pitch to editors.

All the best for 2015

AA

[postcard of Berlinde de Bruyckere's Wound to Simon Wilson]

Ghent, 12.XII.2014

[Berlinde de Bruyckere] show quite gruelling—brilliant but all those pallid, crippled bodies, sutures & bandages made the gallery into a surgical ward. But I think she is the best figure sculptor since Giacometti. Her current show at Hauser & Wirth is a mini replica of the Ghent display. The Musée d'Ixelles [Paul] Delvaux show[40] incl. some erotic drawings and some work new to me—early & mature. Delvaux seems more & more an artist of great diversity & sophistication.

All the best for 2015

A.

39   British poet, curator and art critic Edward Ludie-Smith (b. 1933), wrote the first catalogue article on Adams in 2004.
40   "Paul Delvaux Dévoilé", Musée d'Ixelles, Brussels, 24 October 2014-18 January 2015.

How to Start a Dissident Art Movement

[postcard of Rubens's Venus Frigida to Roger Bates]

Bruxelles → London, 14.XII.2014

This painting was the highlight of the Rubens show (shortly for London).[41] An amazing painting of flesh & skin & hair. Woodcuts, Watteau nude painting & trois crayons drawings also mesmerising. Delvaux show good—still new stuff being shown. B. de Bruyckere had an imposing display in her home city of Ghent. Stayed in Ghent mainly—dodged rail strikes & a royal funeral. Overall a productive but tiring visit. Longing to have a studio again—have a studio again—have lots of ideas for colour paintings and don't really feel at ease except when I am able to paint when I need to. I envy your freedom to work, time permitting. Otherwise, no news. Hope all's well with you.

As ever

A.

[extract of letter to Edward Lucie-Smith]

Cardiff, 23.XII.2014

I liked your new articles but I differ with you about Glenn Brown. I don't think he is much concerned with getting us to spot the references—after all, how many New York gallerists, Hong Kong millionaires and LA society types are going to know Aelst or [Adolph von] Menzel or [Joshua] Reynolds? No, I think the inveterate reference spotters are the dopes who write the catalogues and press releases. Brown genuinely seems to love art that is overlooked and

41   "Sensation and Sensuality: Rubens and His Legacy", *BOZAR*, Brussels, 25 September 2014-4 January 2015; later touring to the Royal Academy, London.

despised (by at least the avant-garde, quasi-avant-garde maybe), and his weird fusions have life because he spots analogies and correspondences between these influences. I don't think it matters much whether or not we get the associations; it is the overall effects he achieves that count. In that sense I think he is different (and superior) [from] other artists of his generation. He is the true inheritor to the Salonistes, just as de Bruyckere is the latest in the line of South Netherlandish, Brabantine and Flemish figure painters and sculptors. Neither of them stand outside the tradition and comment from the sidelines and appropriate to self-aggrandise. At least, that's the way I see it.

Have you seen the Pérez Simón collection at Leighton House?[42] That's pure Glenn Brown—Heliogabalus[43] and all that. I reviewed it for another outlet. It's rather fun.

*[postcard of Diebenkorn city painting to Basil
Beattie]*

London, 18.III.2015

"Diebenkorn" patchy but good overall. *Ocean Park*s rather too dully painted (diluted paint). Definitely worth seeing. Am reviewing it. "Balke" at Nat[ional] Gal[lery] terrible, piss-poor stuff.[44] Just interviewed Ian Davenport re new colour etchings. Next to Paris to review "Bonnard". Still

42   "A Victorian Obsession: The Pérez Simón Collection", Leighton House Museum, London, 14 November 2014-29 March 2015.
43   Roman Emperor, noted for his decadence and for executing individuals under a weight of rose petals, was subject of a number of academic paintings.
44   "Peder Balke", National Gallery, London, 12 November 2014-12 April 2015.

selling v. little, no London dealer interest. Any news?
Regards

AA

[postcard of Bonnard's Place du Clichy to David Lee]

Paris, 21.III.2015

Press dept. most unresponsive—had to queue for ages & pay for entry. Exhibition very crowded & hot. The art is excellent. Really wonderful stuff—sadly, no drawings but top-class paintings. In lightly washed colour a pos. influence of Munch. *La Palme* is fantastic but no duff pictures, In London "Balke" is dreadful—worst non-contemp. show I ever saw at N[ational] G[allery]. Diebenkorn good in places.[45] *Ocean Park* series is weakest in display. I will review that for another outlet. Couldn't face Louvre crowds...

AA

[postcard of Bonnard's Nu dans un intérieur to Basil Beattie]

Cardiff, 3.IV.2015

I read of Bert Irvin's death just now & thought of you.[46] I know that you were close & it must be a sad time for you. I only knew him by sight & said hello to him a couple of times. I hope you aren't doing too badly. Just back from Paris. The "Bonnard" was staggering.[47] The best stuff is

---

45   "Richard Diebenkorn", Royal Academy, London, 14 March-7 June 2015.

46   British abstract painter Albert Irvin (1922-2015) was a close colleague of Beattie. Beattie, Irvin and Bates taught at Goldsmiths College during Adams's time of study there.

47   "Pierre Bonnard: Painting Arcadia", Musée d'Orsay, Paris, 17

electrifying. Well worth a visit, if you can stand the crush. My review is in May's *Jackdaw*. I am finishing a new book: 1 long poem w/ illus. Published early summer.

Thinking of you

AA

[postcard of Bacon's Imaginary Portrait of Pope Pius XII to ER]

Norwich, 5.V.2015

Visited Norwich in E. England to review a show of Bacon & the Masters (Rembrandt, Michelangelo, Ingres, Soutine).[48] Wonderful show & Bacon looks very bold and also considered & serious. Matisses & Soutines great. This region is the mustard-growing area so the fields are the yellow of English mustard. Only my 2nd visit here (first was for my own exhibition here in 1998). Any news on sales or Paris gallery?

Bisous

A. xx

[postcard of Pollock's Number 23 to Basil Beattie]

Liverpool, 3.VII.2015

Some terrific Pollock black paintings in Liverpool now.[49] Hope you will be able to see them. Not a large show but plenty of crackers. Show not too crowded. My review appears in the next *Jackdaw*. I am drawing a lot as I have no studio for painting. No London dealer & no exhibition

March-19 July 2015.
48   "Francis Bacon and the Masters", Sainsbury Centre for Visual Arts, Norwich, 18 April-26 July 2015.
49   "Jackson Pollock: Blind Spots", Tate Liverpool, 30 June-18 October 2015.

plans.

Regards

A.

[postcard of Böcklin's Villa by Sea to Roger Bates]

Frankfurt, 12.VII.2015

The best of Böcklin is truly uncanny. He was by no means overrated by the manic adulation c. 1900. Fantastic Netherlandish paintings, some Romantics, good Beckmanns, lousy recent painting—total shit. Visited Goethe's house, Palmegarten, Zoo & drew model. Hotel in seedy underbelly—huge degradation of drunks on street, meth heads, vagrants smoking crack outside supermarkets, desperate beggars, panhandlers, etc. My Bulgarian model was shocked at the contrast of great wealth & dire poverty. Like a Grosz satire. Terrorist arrested on my plane.

A.

[postcard of Adams's Marta Skłodowska to Brian Sewell]

Bristol, 31.VII.2015

Here is a new drawing. Fernand Khnopff would scorn it, I'm sure. Too much time in Bruxelles Musée fin-de-siècle... Just heard there will be a show of Degas monotypes in NYC summer next year. Would love to visit & review but doubt I would have the cash. Working on new *silverpoint* drawings w/ chalk highlights, pos. for Paris solo show—only my dealer, my paintings. The silverpoints look similar to this drawing, also on coloured grounds. [...] Hope things aren't

too beastly for you.[50]
    Regards

                                                                AA

[extract of letter to Brian Sewell]

                                        Bristol, 10.IX.2015

Currently reviewing Leonardo. I recall you mentioning what a terrible painter he is—I concur, for the late
paintings at least. *The Holy Family, St John & Bacchus* are
repulsive paintings. They make my flesh crawl. But so many
good drawings in the new Milan catalogue. The machine
drawings of Codex Atlanticus so often surprise me. Some
great drawings but he's overrated as a painter though I love
La Belle Ferroniere.

*[postcard of Lithographic Museum, Eindhoven to
Roger Bates]*

                                        Eindhoven, 22.IX.2015

Talked to Gertjan Forrer, master printmaker, & he told
me he met [Barry] Flanagan 3 times in prof. capacity at
the print studio. Twice he (BF) was so paralytically drunk
he couldn't work. That would have been in [Denmark] or
[the Netherlands]. GF worked with many of the COBRA
artists. The lithograph museum here is amazing: great
working presses, giant stones, good examples of artistic &
commercial lithos. OV & I will exhibit together—scratch
display in Coventry. You are welcome to visit. Contact OV
for details. Hope to hear from you soon.

50   Sewell was dying of cancer at this time.

How to Start a Dissident Art Movement

*[letter to Simon Wilson, enclosing copy of On
Dead Mountain]*

Bristol, 20.X.2015

Dear Simon

Enclosed is the second copy, signed but undedicated. Thank
you for the purchases.

I have started an oil painting* of Kolevatov & Yudin
(the front-cover image).[51] It is the first oil painting in a
year. It is half finished and very good. The sky and trees
are almost done. The figures are roughed in but are almost
done. The figures must stay simple while being persuasive
for the image to retain its iconic quality. It must be simple
& memorable to have emotional power. The elaboration
can come in the trees. The image is entirely imaginary so I
feel free and unburdened by a source image. I will make oil
paintings of most of the images in the book. [...] It is wonderful to use impasto and the palette knife again. I started
the painting before I came to London & saw the Auerbach
retrospective but of course I saw the paintings & felt them
in my body, because the muscles retain their memory of
how paint is applied & manipulated.

Many thanks

A.

* 40" x 30"

[extract of letter to Basil Beattie]

Bristol, 28.III.2016

Many thanks for the signed catalogue. There is work there
new to me. The recent paintings of course but also those
small paintings. I love the lushness of the surfaces. Also

51   Two characters in Adams's poem-book *On Dead Mountain*.

one gets a new dynamic when making really small objects. Viewers have a different relationship with objects that are hand/head size and handleable, especially if the materials and marks are relatably scaled. That is, when I saw a Van Eyck saint in Philadelphia on a small panel, I didn't find myself thinking about it much differently to the Ghent Altarpiece but when I see an object that is small but with relatively large marks and strongly tactile in character, I find myself relating to that object quite differently. I'm sure you know what I mean.

[letter to Basil Beattie]

New York City, 16.IV.2016

Dear Basil

Arrived in Manhattan to early spring weather. Walking between museums and galleries. Visited a display of Kirchner—good exhibition but not art I admire—and a terrific Dubuffet show at Acquavella.[52] I was blown away by it— the invention, vitality, diversity, *force*. Art brut is limited but my god it has that energy and impact so little else can match. Dubuffet's early art (the display showed art from 1940s and 1950s) has that raw directness that I really admire. There were wooden driftwood heads—laconic & grotesque. You saw it all 40 years ago, I'm sure, but seeing it en masse is new for me. The selection was very good, including some loans, and the quality in depth intensifies impressions. There is subtlety and delicacy in the textured abstracts. Some of them are lovely and they seem more so when you view them proximate to the forceful figure paintings. All this reminded me of his colleague Asger Jorn's art, which I

52   "Jean Dubuffet: Anticultural Positions", Acquavella Gallery, New York, 15 April–10 June 2016.

saw in depth in Denmark. I admire the same qualities in his art. Previous to this encounter and a display of graphics in Berlin I had a lingering prejudice about Dubuffet because his late work is so poor. People who admire the late stuff don't understand that which makes the early art so strong but all I saw as a student was Dubuffet's late stuff reproduced in magazines. No wonder I disliked him. Now I've seen the best work my view is completely revised.

Walking along West 57th I looked through a lobby window and saw giant Mirós (poor, vacant, showy), a [Morris] Louis pour piece, a terrific [Franz] Kline and a large Balthus (very strong). Also a large Basquiat and an indifferent (but valuable) Diebenkorn *Ocean Parkway*. That's the sort of stuff you just see through a window here.

Tomorrow I see Degas at MoMA and Munch at Neue Galerie.[53] On Wednesday I go to Philadelphia to see the new Barnes Foundation museum—that will include a Picasso exhibition—and Philadelphia Museum, which has Renoir's *Grandes Baigneuses* (one of my favourite paintings) and a beautiful Van Eyck.

On my last day I will view a show of Guston abstracts. I shall review the show and the republished memoir of Guston's daughter for *Jackdaw*. I will send you a copy I know you respond most to his late paintings but I'm curious about your thoughts on his abstract pictures.

Alas the Cedar Tavern closed in 2007 so not even a symbolic visit is possible. But then shouldn't I be seeking out the current places and mixing with today's painters? I don't think I will. There are no painters in NYC. Shan't see any

53   Respectively "Edgar Degas: A Strange New Beauty", MoMA, New York, 26 March-24 July 2016 and "Munch and Expressionism", Neue Galerie, New York, 18 February 18-13 June 2016.

contemporary art while I am here—it would be a waste of time.

18.IV.2016

The Degas is a good show. I am not sure it will be a crowd-pleaser but it's comprehensive and well researched. The general public don't understand what prints are or the challenges that face printmakers. Printmaking is harder than painting or drawing—harder than anything apart from carving—which needs a conceptual intelligence to realise the execution. My review appears in *Burlington Magazine*, June issue.

Great display of MoMA's Pollock art. An early painting *Flame* caught my eye—flame-like drapery folds that Pollock so patiently copied from Michelangelo and El Greco, as Benton taught him. It has real animal energy. The drip paintings look as fine as ever. Great stuff. Solo show in Broodthaers was very poor. Previously I had thought of him as witty and lucid, without knowing his art well. Now I have seen it en masse I conclude he was pretty feeble—except the bones painted in French & Belgian colours, there was nothing worth looking at. Terrific Matisses & Picassos but I saw no Bonnards. Either I missed a hell of a lot of rooms or much of the art was in storage. One Hopper? Surely not. (I don't like Hopper but I know MoMA has more.) No Balthus paintings? Hmmm...

Great Munch show at Neue Galerie. Munch grows the more one sees of him. The Germans—Beckmann excepted—looked histrionic & crude. Fine painting by Gerstl and (early) Kokoschka & drawings by Schiele.

It all gives me lots of ideas.

Best wishes from NYC

AJA

How to Start a Dissident Art Movement

[postcard of New York City to Edward Lucie-Smith]

New York City, 22.IV.2016

Just toured the Whitney Museum. Fuck me! What a waste of time! 8 floors = 1 floor video installation, 1 floor mixed art (1960s-2010s), ½ floor photos. No classic American Modernism, no Ab[stract] Ex[pressionism], no Minimalism, no early C20[th] art. If I'd paid for entry I'd be seething. Even less art here than ARoS in Århus.[54] Time to visit the Met. Going to Washington DC tomorrow. Have plenty of material for 3 articles and an academic paper (Herbert Huncke).

Regards

AA

[postcard of Rothko's Green & Maroon to NL]

Washington DC, 23.IV.2016

Writing this from Nat[ional] Gallery. Saw the Rothkos at Phillips C[ollection]. Very powerful. Like standing in front of a furnace. This painting least aggressive. Rothko can be aggressive/oppressive—deliberately so. I don't state that as criticism. Keen on Bierstadt, Hudson River School & Eakins, which you can't see in Europe. Also the Tonalists. Decent Picassos, interesting Degas portraits (I am here to review his MoMA show) and Ingres's masterly Mme Moitessier. That reminds me to visit the Frick Collection tomorrow, also maybe Brooklyn Museum. Look forward to reading your impressions of NYC art. *Avoid the Whitney!*

A. x

54   Adams wrote a negative review of the art museum at Århus, following an August 2013 visit.

168

[letter to Basil Beattie]

Greenwich Village, New York City,
26.IV.2016

Dear Basil

Just attended opening of "Guston, 1957-1967" at Hauser & Wirth.[55] A really museum-quality exhibition. The paintings of the period are lush and broadly brushed—very sensual, the most tactile and delicious of all his paintings. 36 paintings and a wall of framed drawings, uniform size, simple, sparse. All good stuff, including loans from museums. In one you can see the paint go over the stretcher edge, showing that he painted canvas unstretched and tacked to a wall (which I already knew). Have you tried painting that way since 1988? Would that approach work with your current forms? If you have a chance to see the show, I recommend it. It closes 29 July. It has a full catalogue—which I haven't yet seen—which is an alternative to travelling.

At the gallery I had a chance to speak to Musa Mayer, Guston's daughter. I told her how her father's example had liberated you when you felt stymied and needed to use recognisable images and symbols. I also said that you had spoken of this to your students and thereby passed on Guston's liberation and brave example to the next generation. She was very pleased to hear it and said that she felt her father's flame was passed on.

Now sitting outside the Ear Inn in Greenwich Village, waiting for a friend. Flying home tonight so I think I'll post this in England. Weather broken cloud and chance of storms.

There's nothing much to be added, so I'll end here and post this when I arrive in England tomorrow.

55   26 April-29 July 2016.

Best wishes

Alexander

[extract of letter to Simon Wilson]

Bristol, 4.VI.2016

The discussion in *RA Magazine* is evenly balanced. You are both right. Critics should be negative when the art is weak *and* the claims for it are unreasonable (no writer should savage an amateur, even one showing publicly) but the best criticism is to ignore. I never review an artist unless I consider him to be at least my equal or better than me except when I need an example in a wider argument (e.g. [Richard] Hamilton in a discussion of the inanity of Conceptual art). I simply won't waste my time (or that of my readers) on weak art, which is why I don't review contemporary art. Also, how is one to counter the idiocy & puffery of curators, dealers and academics unless one destroys their arguments (and, as collateral damage, their artists)? One needs to keep idiocy in check somehow—especially if those idiots are powerful and influential and their idiocy adversely affects critical standards.

[postcard of Bacon's Women to Simon Wilson]

Liverpool, 28.VIII.2016

Now in Liverpool. Best thing in show[56] is the Hirshhorn triptych—I shall mention something curious about sex in my review. The Stedelijk *Woman & Child* is very highly and delicately coloured. Sadly, a lot of green paintings (from Germany)—pretty ropey. Good show overall. Liked the 1988 orange painting—precursor to 1990 triptych. Hudder-

---

56   "Francis Bacon: Invisible Rooms", Tate Liverpool, 18 May–18 September 2016.

sfield figure also good to see again. Now off to Manchester to work with a model then to Bristol. Heap of reviews to write. Ideas for landscapes (French, Monegasque) + nudes (stripes).

A.

[Bacon postcard to Roger Bates]

Manchester, 28.VIII.2016

Wending my way back to Bristol. Monaco – Nice – Liverpool – Manchester – Cardiff – Bristol. Saw Bacon shows in Monaco[57] and Liverpool. Great art but a ridiculous performance. Lost my jacket & house keys, bank card refused, flight delayed, shoes had holes. Down & out in Monaco. Doing all this on the unfounded expectation of perhaps making something back. Absurd gamble—and Monte Carlo is the place for those. Hope all is well with you.

Best wishes

AA

[letter to OV, written on reverse of AA review of
Francis Picabia]

Bristol, 9.IX.2016

Dear O.

Thought this might amuse you. My thesis is that Modernism was cut short by Post-Modernism. Post-Modernism has been taken up with alacrity by anti-Modernists. Thus remaining strands of Modernism (abstract painting, process painting, sculpture & painting highly formalist in content) is under fire from PM and trad. advocates. I see

---

57   "Francis Bacon: Monaco and French Culture", Grimaldi Forum, Monaco, 2 July-4 September 2016.

both you and I as Late Modernists.

PM is viable if deployed as by Picabia—the truly rootless, unprogrammatic, non-ironic artist—that is, if PM approach is entirely subordinated to the content of the individual work of art and its inherent qualities then PM can be successful. In practice I can't remember anyone except Picabia doing that, hence I consider him the only *real* PM artist and the only *successful* PM artist. Most (all other?) PM artists turn art into a game of "spot the reference"—thus the only function of their art is non-formal. That is their PM art becomes null because all formal elements (technique, form, process) become neutered to allow the extra-formal elements (reference, humour, quote) to function. Thus their art is hollow and formally null. It is the negation of art because fine art can only exist in formal plastic terms not extraneous ones. It is destructive and it ultimately short-circuits fine art because PM art says "nothing matters here; art has no formal qualities".
Perhaps that does not come through in this short review. One would have to read 10 pieces by me to understand this position. Ah well...

Write soon!

A.

[postcard of Adams's Marta Skłodowska to OV]

Bristol, 12.IX.2016

Actually I would add Magritte's Vache paintings[58] as examples of successful PM painting (so, proto-PM) but Picabia's range, subjects and tone are more varied, unexpected and effective. Vache is more coherent as a body but Picabia's

---

58   The brief Vache (Fr: cow) period of René Magritte was characterised by a wild heterogenous style and anarchic humour. See Alexander Adams, Magritte, Prestel, Munich, 2022, p. 84.

paintings are stronger individually & more memorable, also P. is a better demonstration of PM's potential. They are both good painters & better than today's.

Yours

A.

[postcard of Pollock's Bue Poles to Basil Beattie]

Bristol, 1.X.2016

I'm sure you'll see the Ab. Ex. show at the RA but just writing to recommend it.[59] Some terrific paintings. Some terrific paintings. *Blue Poles* looks better than I had thought it. *Mural* (newly restored) looks fabulous—bursting with energy, hypnotic. The late purely abstract de Koonings are stunningly lush and rich. Thought Gottlieb was underrepresented; Frankenthaler very poor, but [I am] knowledgeable about her work. I will send you the review when it is published (end of Oct.). No other news—just not selling art, writing & publishing some stories.

Regards

A.

[extract of letter to Simon Wilson]

Bristol, 19.XI.2016

I'm glad you noted my words on Rothko. I find them very powerful—even aggressive—works. I had a friend who was very sensitive (to art and in general) and he couldn't go near Rothkos because of the sense of space, heat and light they engendered. He found them very unnerving and I must say I increasingly see his viewpoint. The correlation between high colour and gaiety is facile and largely inaccurate. It

59   "Abstract Expressionism", Royal Academy, London, 24 September 2016-2 January 2017.

is also connected to the Sublime—that feeling of encountering the unearthly and illimited in a way that bypasses reason. Opening yourself up to such an experience can be unmanning and I don't at all blame my friend for not feeling able to confront the challenge. I don't doubt that some of Rothko's urges were driven by anger and religious ecstasy and even malice. You find that with Serra, in his tilted pieces. The weight could kill spectators and that fear informs how we react to that art—we read it in a bodily way. And I am absolutely sure that Serra understands this and uses it consciously to inform his practice. He means to threaten us, just as he means to dominate a plaza (see *Tilted Arc* etc.). Rothko means to transport us, but also to unsettle us, to make us afraid. And he succeeds. That is also what I understand as the Sublime—to transport the viewer with overwhelming emotion. Rothko is the least decorative painter who ever lived. [Clyfford] Still also falls into this area by oppressing us with huge scale. But I suspect Still does this to cover up weaknesses and doubts in himself. If you know anything of the man—intransigent, hectoring, grand, bombastic—you know he was compensating for inner doubt. I don't go in for psychological profiling of artists but with Still you can see the old-time Puritan unwilling to allow a scintilla of doubt to creep into his mind or that of his audience. He is an extremist and all extremists are attempting to smother a fear of chaos and unpredictability. Now, I don't say that diminishes Still as an artist but it makes me think his motivation is internal and psychological rather than intellectual or aesthetic. I am wary of artists who intimidate their viewers—physically or intellectually.

And as I said, dismissing Rothko is daft. Reduction of motifs doesn't equal lack of content and high colour doesn't equal lack of seriousness. But anyone who dismisses abstract art as a whole is more impressed by their own obstinacy than anything they encounter in the world around them. [...]

Researching Leighton.[60] Don't know what to make of him. Sometimes I get the feeling that I am overlooking something very essential and profound—some sort of lesson taken from his life and work—and other times I wonder if he was just a competent but erratic Aesthetic painter. Should I be looking behind the mask for something or is the lesson that I should be looking at the mask alone, for that is all there is? It isn't that I feel L. is insincere or some sort of trick is being played. I haven't made some great investment of passion, time or advocacy on L.'s behalf. I just wonder if some important truth will reveal itself to me and how long I might have to hang around before deciding there is no truth forthcoming. It is like those magic-eye matrices. Stare long enough and the hidden image will reveal itself. I've been staring at Leighton for months and all I can see are the dots—the constituent parts—but no hidden image has appeared and maybe there is none to be seen.

[extract of letter to OV]

Bristol, 5.XII.2016

The show of Jason Martin was good.[61] I liked the restraint, as the paintings were sombrely coloured and the subdued colour offset the powerful gestures. A balance. The large paintings are painted different colours, layer over layer, wet on wet. Then the paint is smoothed with a plasterer's float (the catalogue writer says "trowel" but I've done more plastering than him). Then Martin disrupts the paint by brushing vigorously crossways (vertical format, horizontal

60   Lord Frederic Leighton (1830-1896), Aesthetic painter, was subject of several reviews by Adams.
61   "Jason Martin", Lisson Gallery, London, 18 November 2016-7 January 2017. Martin (b. 1970) studied at Goldsmiths College 1990-3.

marks) and that brings out the lower levels. But he doesn't work it over too hard so it feels fresh and there's some spatter. Very ruminative works, action painting notwithstanding. Not sure if it is Process Painting or not. It's a hybrid, maybe. Martin, [Callum] Innes & [Ian] Davenport are all doing good painting and [Ian] McKeever & Beattie of the older generation are also doing well. (McKeever's photo assemblages seem to have been a passing phase. They aren't as effective as his pure paintings.) Will review JM for *British Art Journal*. Angela de la Cruz[62] has a show at Lisson next year. I'll review that also. I chided the press officer about JM & AdlC not having enough shows in London and she said, "That's the difficulty with having 52 artists". I wanted to reply that was the gallery's fault but just said I was only interested in JM & AdlC. She tried to interest me in some other artist and I evaded. 52 artists and only 2 good ones. Good grief!

[postcard of Adams's Firs in Snow to Simon Wilson]

Bristol, 19.XII.2016

Yes, considering Watts Gallery.[63] Why not? (Except I don't like the stuff.) Would be a slog getting there. Would have to append as spur to a stay in London. Perhaps not too expensive as day-return by rail (from London). Re narrative— why not change? Kafka started *Das Schloß* in first person and later changed to 3rd. Might free you. I can't write in first person (except letters). Also, in narrative prose, I don't want readers thinking they are seeing *me*. All they'll see is some distant approximation so best to give them "A.".

62   Spanish painter Angela de la Cruz (b. 1965) studied at Goldsmiths College 1991-4.
63   Museum of Victorian painter G.F. Watts (1817-1904).

Less confusion.

A.

[letter to Basil Beattie]

Bristol, 20.XII.2016

Dear Basil

Am currently reading the new biography of Kafka by Reiner Stach (3 volumes, Princeton University Press). My review will appear on *Spiked* website, probably in late January. I cannot recommend the biography highly enough. It really isn't too dense and if one has a knowledge of (and love for) Kafka then it is an easy read. Stach says so many intelligent things about Kafka's life and writings but is not presumptuous on matters of interpretation—very intelligent, informed, fair, scrupulously researched. Every page reminds me why I love Kafka so deeply and how important he is to me. Kafka is—for me—the greatest, truest, most powerful of all writers—any era, any culture. If you read biographies, please seek this out.

Best wishes for 2017

Alexander

[extract of letter to Mary Ann Caws[64]]

Bristol, 3.I.2017

I recently read your book *Robert Motherwell: With Pen and Brush*[65] and enjoyed it. I found it illuminating and informative. I have always considered Motherwell underrated. I reviewed the catalogue raisonné for *The Art Newspaper*

64   American art historian and academic, Mary Ann Caws (b. 1933).
65   Reaktion Books, London, 2004.

when it was published. I had two thoughts about your book which might be of use or interest to you.

There is an extended quote on pp. 82-3 where Motherwell mentions the alleged advice Goya gave. The quote as you gave it is as follows: "They say that Goya always 'finished' his pictures by candlelight, i.e., in dim light. I understand that. Subtle minor adjustments are critical to the feeling of the pictures as a whole…" I don't have my copy of *Collected Writings* to hand, so I don't know what followed that ellipsis. I assume that Motherwell's interpretation of Goya's advice is as presented in your quote (that is, there are no qualifiers that follow). If so, Motherwell is entirely wrong about Goya's thinking, which I find startling as I have always considered Motherwell an astute commenter. As a painter who has often followed Goya's advice, I can tell you that Goya's meaning in contrary to how Motherwell understood it. In half-light the eye has difficulty calculating half-tones and details. In general, a painting develops from the bold to the fine, the rough to the detailed, towards exactitude. This has a tendency to drain energy and impact from a painting. Goya understood that towards the end of the painting process the artist gets obscured by finishing touches, detail, finessing finish. Therefore, Goya suggested to painters that they end in half-light because it forces the painter to add bold touches which enliven a painting and counteract that daintiness. You judge the overall impression of projection/recession and tonal contrast and adjust accordingly. One paints "subtle minor adjustments" (by which I understand Motherwell to mean details) in full light. Either I have misunderstood Motherwell's meaning or Motherwell has misapprehended Goya's advice.

[letter to Simon Wilson]

Bristol, 9.I.2017

Dear Simon

"Taste is the death of art" according to Sickert, as you write. Well, yes. I understand Sickert to mean that questions of taste drive viewers away from strong and exciting art due to considerations of morality and beauty—or more perhaps immorality and ugliness. I suppose he also meant that considerations of taste can cause an artist to blunt his approach or relinquish a subject he thinks will be deemed unacceptable by his audience. That's true enough, as far as it goes. I had an additional and different point. Mine was that if considerations of taste at all then the art is deficient. It is not a matter of whether artist and audience alter their views or openness in response to considerations of taste. My point is that if the consideration is raised at all then there is a problem. To my mind the greatest art transcends all consideration of taste because it has compulsive emotional force, perfection, evokes the sensation of the sublime. Naturally, very little art is on this level so it is perhaps not a fair or workable criterion with which to judge art. One cannot expect a Boudin beach view or a Diebenkorn still-life to overwhelm one with transcendent emotion but they are fine examples of art nevertheless. But my dictum goes: if considerations of taste come up when looking at art then that art is faulty, insincere or mediocre. I don't say it is bad art, simply that it is second rate at least and maybe worse or even worthless. *Le Radeau de la Méduse* cannot be judged by taste because it has force so powerful that taste never seems relevant or important and—in my case—I never considered the moral case for/against the painting. It all ties into my idea of the greatest art being sublime.

So although I agree with Sickert, my thesis is different

and more far reaching than his observation. My point is to do with the comprehension and perception of art at its highest level. I don't deal with taste in my writing—except in Leighton—because by and large I discuss art at a higher level. And when I deal in passing with a very minor artist—like Pascin[66]—it doesn't seem very useful to expend 50 words on morality rather than simply introducing the artist, subject and technique. I only discussed taste in relation to Picabia because the critics do. Ah, you say—if anyone raises the subject at all then the art must be deficient according to your rule. Well, I suppose so. I write that Picabia is a brilliant painter and the best of all post-Modernists because he has no irony, he is genuinely rootless. But I never suggested all his paintings were great. I suppose he has good pictures and better and worse ones. He can be slight but not trite. Judged on his weaker pieces one inevitably thinks about taste, vulgarity, banality. Looking at *Worship of the Calf*, one doesn't think of these matters.

Actually, the reason Pascin sprang to mind (Barnes Foundation review) is because he was one of those rare cases where I did comment on the air of sordidness, dissipation and loucheness. That is because that side is his most prominent one and a characteristic feature of his art. He is also an undeniably minor artist. So, as such he is the prime example where moral/taste judgments come into one's thoughts. If I review the big Rodin show in Paris (March)—I doubt it—I wouldn't mention vulgarity in relation to *Iris* because the consideration wouldn't come to mind.

Regarding Berger.[67] I think dealing with him in half a

---

66   Bulgarian Jules Pascin (1885-1930), minor École de Paris artist noted for his erotic scenes.
67   British Marxist art critic John Berger had recently died. Adams wrote an obituary that was rejected for publication.

paragraph at the end of the Julian Barnes review ([*The Jack-daw*] no. 122, p. 39) is all that was needed.

For the next *Jackdaw* I will cover Cagnacci and Sebastiano del Piombo. Also supposed to write an online review of Bouchardon books—only if the publisher will send 90-gbp-worth of books for a website review. There is something rather curious that will surface, in March I guess. Of course, you'll hear about it from me.

Well, I'm all written out about taste and I can't believe the hours I've expended on Berger—hours I'll never get back. What a waste!

Herzlichen Grüßen![68]

A.

[extract of letter to BW]

Bristol, 22.I.2017

Only last week I found an envelope you posted in April—containing Signac information. Many (belated) thanks for that! The man must have [had] the patience of a saint to work in such a way. I once tried making a Pointillist painting and I gave up before completing it. The rigid, scientific approach to painting—especially in such a restrictive, repetitive and time-consuming manner—is quite alien to me. However, I hugely admire Seurat and always get a thrill from his work. Signac never provokes that reaction in me. He is competent and intelligent and diligent but I think a great artist needs more than that. Perhaps he doesn't need intelligence; it often gets in the way. Good judgment, good instincts, yes. Analytical detachment? No. Or at least that is optional.

68   German: Heartfelt greetings.

How to Start a Dissident Art Movement

[extract of letter to LV]

Bristol, 31.V.2017

I am just back from the Raphael drawing exhibition at the Ashmolean, Oxford.[69] I am reviewing it for *The Jackdaw*. It is wonderful—some great treasures. As an artist, I marvelled at his skill and intelligence. I wish he had drawn some landscapes. It would have been fascinating to see how he might have treated views. Will you have a chance to visit?

At the moment I am drawing large landscapes on textured paper. The weave of the paper and organic quality of the surface interacts with the drawn marks. That gives them an added richness. My subjects are a park in south Wales and the Jardin japonaise in Monaco. There is also a wonderful view of banana trees next to an apartment building and a view of sea seen below a road flyover.

[postcard of Soutine's Butcher Boy to Roger Bates]

London, 7.XI.2017

In London to review Soutine, *Monochrome* and Whiteread.[70] All good shows. Whiteread felt a little lightweight but some lovely objects there. Drawings poor. You'll read my Soutine & *Monochrome* reviews. This Soutine is terrific—like a demon butcher wrenched out of hell by his eye socket. Some really lovely paintwork & sensitive portrayals. Bought some tinted Ingres paper for drawing from Shepherd's. Too good

69   "Raphael: The Drawings", Ashmolean Museum, Oxford, 1 June-3 September 2017.

70   Respectively "Soutine's Portraits: Cooks, Waiters & Bellboys", Courtauld Gallery, 19 October 2017-21 January 2018, "Monochrome: Painting in Black and White" National Gallery, 30 October 2017-18 February 2018 and "Rachel Whiteread", Tate Britain, 12 September 2017-21 January 2018. All of which Adams reviewed.

for letters, alas!

    Yours undercoverly

X. Smada

[extract of letter to OV]

Bristol, 9.XI.2017

I was in the lair of the beast this week. I went to [Tate Britain] to see the Whiteread show. It had some great pieces but the show curation was a mess. I'll send you my review when it is published. Made me kind of melancholic for the early 90s and *House* and a time when the Turner Prize was important and included strong art. Also saw the Soutine (wonderful) and the monochrome show at the [National Gallery]—which has serious problems but is worth seeing, especially for you. Again, I'll post you a copy of the review when published. Some of the abstract paintings shouldn't have been included, though the Stella and [Josef] Albers are real gems. They are graphic duotone works not grisailles, which are the subject of the show and are comprised of art made in shades of grey, black and white. The duotone works function on aesthetic and conceptual levels very dissimilar to those of the grisaille works. I suspect the curators lost their nerve and included these works to draw a more diverse crowd. I'll be back in London soon and will review the Modigliani.

[letter to Roger Bates]

Bristol, 21.XII.2017

Dear Roger

Thanks for the card. I assume mine arrived some time ago.

    A pull-quote from me in *The Visitors' Book*? I haven't seen it. Publishers don't ask permission to quote and don't send copies or photocopies, so I have no idea what quotes by me are circulating. [...] Next time I'm in a book store I'll take a look.

Yes, [Francis] Bacon seems to have been a tyrant in private—playing power games, humiliating friends, demanding loyalty, excommunicating friends and so on. He could be generous with time and money but I confess if I had a friend like that we wouldn't be friends for very long. Did you read Peppiatt's *Bacon in your Blood* and Farson's biography of FB? They both also document Bacon's monstrous generosity. As for his art, I contend that it was outright bad c. 1956-62 in the transitional period, rather dry and repetitive c. 1974-84 and otherwise very consistent and strong. c. 850 paintings isn't that many for a career c. 1930 (actually c. 1940)-1992. FB was fairly fastidious about production though some very poor art did seep out—not much though. One aspect he was very good on was *space*. The way he used pictorial devices as quasi-spatial markers is really wonderful and not talked about enough. The exploration of areas as abstract design, flat surface and depicted space is really exciting and rewarding and it's one of the parts that has influenced me most.

Which aspects of FB do you like/dislike? Or is it a matter of good and bad pictures or subjects or periods?

Best to both of you

A.

[extract of letter to Roger Bates]

Bristol, 16.IV.2018

Just completed a series of colour paintings, all of Sweden. It involved underpainting then overpainting and some glazes. I painted the first coat as complementary to the top coat; that gives the colour density and richness. Here is one example. *Birches and conifers in snow.* These paintings are on canvas board.

It's something to acquaint yourself again with the characteristics of different pigments after two decades of using lamp black and titanium white. Mind you, I don't think any painter forgets how loathsome synthetic ultramarine is (as a material rather than a colour). It turns out that cobalt blue and viridian dries in a couple of hours. I had purchased a few hundred pounds' worth of colour paint so it only cost me the price of the boards. It's time consuming to paint in stages and mix colours and so forth. The fact that I decided to work in groups and variants meant that it was an efficient approach to mix colours which could be used in multiple paintings. The paintings range from the successful to peculiar. There is one painting of a moonlit landscape that is in the style of Van Gogh. Perhaps it is a pastiche, using directional broken brushstrokes. The most effective aspect of the painting is the use of cobalt blue on the snow and ultramarine on the sky. The trees are warm green and dark blue. The only touch of warm colour is the yellow lamplight in the lower window—with a touch of reflection on the snow below that window. The red ground below the blue really generates a frisson. Still, it's only a pastiche.

Debating making larger versions but I suspect these paintings succeed—in as far as they do—only because the images are compressed. Making versions large would be too strong, I suspect. The intensity comes from the juxtaposition of strong colour in close proximity in a small picture. I might try one experiment at medium size.

I'm using a thinner called "Zest-it"—a citrus-scented solvent. It must have degraded because it smells just like white spirit and it dries so slowly you could almost call it a drying retardant. [...] Using Roberson glaze medium—several years old but just fine. Most of the oil paints I had in college are usable—a few have turned solid. It feels good to be using old materials.

Paris paintings all complete. Some sent, others to follow. Catalogue being printed. My dealer wants to add a few gouaches because she fears the prices of the oils will be too much for her collectors. [...] The vernissage will be on 16 May. I will be there for a few days extra in order to visit some museums.

[extract of letter to Basil Beattie]

Bristol, 22.V.2018

I recently returned from Paris. There is an exhibition of Motherwell paintings from the Open series. 17 paintings from the estate. There are some really fine pieces and the central gallery is like a museum display. The exhibition is at Galerie Templon, Paris, until 21 July. I reviewed his catalogue raisonné some years ago. At the time I was a touch sceptical about the Open paintings. They seemed a touch slight. When I saw them first hand, they felt well judged. Of course, there are weak pieces. He doesn't find a way to handle black paintings with the Open motif but the *Spanish Window*, *Dover Beach* and the bronze painting from 1974 are really fine pieces—strong, striking, energetic, richly coloured, spatially deep. They are really wonderful pieces.

Perhaps you feel you've seen your fill of Motherwell over the years, but if you have a chance to go to Paris, I'd recommend a visit. There's also a good Tintoretto show at Musée du Luxembourg open until 1 July.

[postcard of Bruegel's Drunk forced into a Pigsty to David Lee]

Vienna, 3.X.2018

The Bruegel show in Vienna is stunning.[71] Biggest show of his work ever. Wonderful drawings. A few new works, including this, which is a corker! As the Frick is closed, their Bruegel grisaille is here. Shame the Courtauld's couldn't likewise travel. This will be my main review—with you next week. Will see Leopold Museum & Monet at the Albertina but probably just for my review website. *Art Newspaper* may use my ICA letter. Any responses from your contacts? Will let you know if I get any meaningful replies. Barbican, 13 Oct. will be my most public statement on the matter.

AA

[letter to Roger Bates]

Bristol, 14.II.2019

Dear Roger

Saw the Bert Irvin exhibition at the RWA today.[72] You'll see the review in *The Jackdaw* (this or next). Mixed feelings. Some fascinating art—esp. by others, incl. Kitchen Sink painters, Pollock, de Kooning, Sam Francis, Basil Beattie. There is an interview with Basil about Bert in the catalogue. Good piece, which covers teaching at Goldsmiths, St Katharine's Dock, etc. I warmed more to Irvin's art of the 1950s and 1960s—Kitchen Sink and St Ives/Ab. Ex. Styles. The Colour Field stuff of the 1970s left me cold. The late stuff...

71   "Bruegel – Once in a Lifetime", Kunsthistorisches Museum, Vienna, 2 October 2018-13 January 2019.
72   "Albert Irvin and Abstract Expressionism", Royal West of England Academy, Bristol, 8 December 2018-3 March 2019.

well, it seems pretty much Foyer School. I didn't care for it and that will show in the review. Sadly, I had to cut the discussion comparing Irvin and Pollock from my review due to the necessity of keeping it under 500 words. The comparison explained my objections to Irvin's late style. Despite my reservations the last room looks fantastic. Centrepiece is a large painting loaned by Goldsmiths. There's no denying the decorative quality of the late canvases and I don't honestly think my objections are *purely* coolness towards decorative fine art. You can judge from my review.

I sent Basil a postcard mentioning my review. Do you hear from him? I presume you rarely travel to London. (Photos in exhibition of Bert & Betty at Chelsea Fine Art Club.) Any particular memories of Bert? I never met him though Basil's students visited his shows at his London gallery in the early '90s and he was working at Advanced Graphics at the same time as me. I had chances to meet him but I don't really "collect" artist[s] in that way. Also I didn't much like the late work so I couldn't imagine what I would have said to him, though I'm sure it would have been a pleasant enough encounter.

[*Culture War*] crawls towards publication. Awaiting reviews.

How are you doing? Any news?

Reviews: Tintoretto, Japanese women in art, Picasso Blue & Rose periods, David Jones, architecture. Soon visiting London to speak at a school. Expect to visit Dorothea Tanning show at Tate Modern for *Jackdaw* review.

Yours ever

A.

[postcard of Krasner's Composition to Basil Beattie]

London, 4.VII.2019

Terrific Krasner exhibition.[73] The Little Image paintings are cracking. Tiny gemlike specks of colour in black webs. Late stuff weak—very thin. Show worth seeing. Also in London to Vallotton, Grosvenor School print (Dulwich), Cindy Sherman and Bacon (Gagosian). Bacon show wonderful. Mainly good picture, lots of space. Includes *The Wrestlers*. Finishing new book on art. Hope you are well.

AA

[extract of letter to Simon Wilson]

Bristol, 1.I.2020

Just listened to a talk on philosopher Julius Evola, Italian aristocrat who developed theories incorporating mysticism, paganism and nationalism into an approach that was aristocratic, hierarchical, anti-liberal, anti-populist. He was the only serious thinker to critique fascism from the right, despising fascism's materialism, socialism and collectivism. He advocated the warrior-priest as the natural leader of nations. This seems to overlap with aspects of Bataille. Curiously, Evola made some Dadaist art/non-art. He said he did it because he opposed bourgeois aesthetics. So at least one Dadaist member/participant/follower was attacking the status quo from a rightist perspective, which I'll admit I'd never previously heard of. Of course, the Futurists did the same but I'd always seen the Dadaists as nihilists, libertarians or socialists/anarchists.

73   "Lee Krasner: Living Colour", Barbican Centre, London, 30 May-1 September 2019.

How to Start a Dissident Art Movement

Bristol, 18.V.2020

Undecided on A[lan] Davie—I like the roughness, primalness and air of early Pollock—but I do harbour doubts about empty calligraphy. You know what I mean? The appearance of symbolism but without the substance. Sound and fury signifying nothing. Well, the appearance of drama is stimulating in itself. I concur re Hockney. I missed Basil's shows of early works in London galleries in Feb. When I went to London for the only time this year I had only time for Beardsley, Spilliaert and Shepherd's paper shop and had to skip the Beatties (even if the shows were open in March).

[extract of letter to Simon Wilson]

Bristol, 20.VIII.2020

On page 5 of Feaver's *Freud* and already I hate it.[74] What a slog! All those fucking anecdotes. Aristocracy with stupid nicknames, rackety debs, pranging luxury cars, screwing fashion models. Now I know why people become Socialists. (Orwell on Socialists hating success, money + the working class.) I reviewed vol. I for *Art Newspaper* and now I'm finishing the job, in more ways than one.

[letter to Roger Bates]

Bristol, 7.IX.2020

Dear Roger

Thanks for your new comments. I was glad you found my Colston piece on point. I suppose there will be opposing

---

74   William Feaver, Lucian Freud: Fame, 1968–2011, Bloomsbury, London, 2020.

views, but my argument is largely covered by my article and the new book. (Thanks for the cheque—expect signed copy soon.)

Regarding [Martin] Parr, I am not sure I wrote that. I recall just forwarding the piece to [David] Lee but I do agree with the sentiments expressed. It is sad that Parr subjected himself to such humiliation. It may be that the publisher and/or Parr's gallerist may have leaned on him. He'll win over nobody with a pro forma confession of his political unorthodoxy. His "transgression" will be held over his head by his supposed political-cultural allies, to be used at their pleasure. With his apology he's debased himself. What a wretched abjection. Better to stand firm.[75] Eventually we'll all get "cancelled"—not least the political enforcers—so one might as well get it over with. Of course, for some (with public-service positions) being cancelled means losing your job and the ability to find one. The culture of fearful silence dominates universities. Goldsmiths Library has announced it is "decolonising" its contents. I suspect all meaningful education would cease in that case, so I don't think the threat will be fully implemented. Horrid prospect! Imagine being a student or member of staff in such a prison colony. Oh, the memoirs to be written by future escapees... I would write a dystopian novel if I had a publisher—it couldn't match reality. You heard that the director of the [British Museum] put founder Sloane's bust into a cabinet where it is shamed by derogatory "contextualisation". Next stage is smashing it while chanting "black lives matter".

Yours dystopianly

A.

75   British photographer Martin Parr (b. 1952) had been accused of racism regarding an image in a book to which he had contributed; he consequently issued an apology.

*[letter to Roger Bates enclosed with copy of
Iconoclasm]*

Bristol, 8.IX.2020

Dear Roger

Delighted to enclose one of the first copies of *Iconoclasm*. It won't be officially published until 6 Oct., so you have a preview. Responses welcome. Apologies if the book tends to incorporate too much previously published material. It seems to form a fairly solid line of argument and I haven't significantly altered my outlook on the topic. The only matter I'm ambivalent regarding is contextualisation. I leave it open as an option but personally regard it with distain, as I consider it a form of public, authority-sanctioned posthumous humiliation. However, if it is the difference between saving and losing a statue, I consider it a price that can be paid—until it can be removed.

    Best wishes

Alex

*[letter to Simon Wilson enclosed with copy of
Iconoclasm]*

Bristol, 9.IX.2020

Dear Simon

Here is the new book signed to you, with thanks. When I skim read it, it seemed like 50% of the text had disappeared. I did have to edit out a lot but not 50%. Just a standard response of disappointment at how cursory and superficial the book seems when compared to my aspirations.

    Glad you like the new drawing. When I get through the glut of sending off books, I shall get down to painting.

    Did you know some gallerist contacted me out of the blue to authenticate his Picasso? I didn't respond more than a polite acknowledgement. If he's asking for my imprimatur that tells you all you need to know about the painting's authenticity.

Regards

A.

[letter to Michael Sandle[76]]

Bristol, 24.XI.2020

Dear Michael

A few extra thoughts. I'm glad participants put their cards on the table and also glad I stirred up some viewers.[77] They've never heard anyone criticise BLM and oppose critical race theory. They simply don't encounter such views and don't permit into their circles anyone who might offer determined questioning. However, I got some private messages of support. It is telling that even within our chat, participants chose to support me in *private*. It demonstrates the crushing suffocation of conformity within our circles which—in our level (as artists)—should be lively and diverse in viewpoints. I'm not at all surprised that I was effectively being heckled and that there were calls to silence me. Some people are terribly entitled and awfully fragile—because they've browbeaten dissidents in their circles into silence. They've never had to argue for their positions/assumptions. Good thing I'm not part of their circles!

It was good to have an artist of your stature to contrib-

76   British sculptor Michael Sandle RA (b. 1936) wrote the introduction to Adams's Iconoclasm, Identity Politics and the Erasure of History (2020).
77   Sandle had presided over an online conference in which Adams participated. Adams had been critical of the destruction of statues over the summer of 2020.

ute. Your works will really last. Jennings is good in his way and I have a lot of respect for him. Sabin Howard seems very competent & dedicated.[78] Mind you, I'm glad that I generally foreswear reviewing living artists—a handful of abstract painters, Serra, that's about it. I don't want to end up a tipster like [Clement] Greenberg, although I admire CG a lot. Formalism has a lot to recommend it, from a critical standpoint. Perhaps you have differing thoughts about Formalism. Have you written any reviews? I wish I had more time for art making.

I do appreciate our dialogue. Being locked up under house arrest is rather lousy—and unfair. "Someone must have been telling lies, for one fine morning Josef K. was arrested." Even my little life-drawing group is dispersed and the dockside pub where it met is closed and dark. Grim tidings... Never mind.

Best wishes

Alexander

[extract of letter to Simon Wilson]

Bristol, 24.XI.2020

I hope to end [my forthcoming book on Magritte] with *Le Dernier Cri*, with a peroration that Magritte is not a proto-Pop artist but a *Romantic* artist. [...] Yes, here's my line of attack—Magritte's position as a proto-Pop artist is a confection of mid-century supporters of Pop who were looking to legitimise their movement. M. was caustic about Pop and wrote/painted in terms that align him with *Romanticism* and in opposition to Pop. It is unlikely that my little picture book will alter perceptions of Magritte but I have very strong feelings on this and want to distance

---

78   Italian-American monumental sculptor Sabin Howard (b. 1963). Adams later interviewed and profiled him.

RM from Pop. I'll give Pop a thorough kicking while I'm at it. Rather than a shifting admixture of admiration/repudiation for mass production that one finds in Pop art, one finds in Magritte a yearning to address eternal human drives towards identification within the natural world and the sublime. I can't think of a greater dichotomy than Pop and Romanticism, with Magritte falling strongly within the latter tendency.

[extract of letter to Simon Wilson]

Bristol, 3.XII.2020

Just re-read Gablik's *Magritte*[79], as research for my own book. Very disappointed. Very baggy, too much junk about Pop, intellectually undisciplined—that's aside from errors of fact, which are somewhat forgiveable, as it was an early book. I had remembered it fondly but upon re-purchasing the book (I couldn't find my original copy), I discovered how faulty my youthful critical faculties must have been. [...] I want to change the way people see RM—a Romantic operating through Surrealism, that's my vision of [Magritte]. Anyway, we'll see if I can back up my thesis.

[extract of letter to OV]

Bristol, 4.V.2021

About the gloss paintings lacking surface incident—other than minimal differences in facture—don't forget [Ad] Reinhardt, but yes, I get your point. A good picture should have a hook, something to catch the eye, engage the imagination, generate frisson, etc. I've destroyed pictures for blandness and conventionality—not quite what you mention but an aesthetic or pictorial blankness equivalent

79   Suzi Gablik, *Magritte*, Thames & Hudson, London, 1970.

to your criticism of pictures. I find your fastidiousness admirable but I can see how it has impeded your creativity and career. Maybe you could take up a series of small pieces as challenges—five-finger exercises. Boxes with gloss, building layers of paint, objects of folded paper or sheet metal, paint on glass—physical things, small, inexpensive, disposable. Just get in and play and see what you learn. It sounds like you're overthinking things and getting fixated on *making art.* Try experimenting and perhaps you'll find something that excites you and you can refine, intellectualise/conceptualise and make into art. Lack of motivation indicates lack of excitement and engagement regarding your motifs and modus operandi. Moving to a different approach is not a retreat or admission of failure. Everything you have done has taken you to where you are now. I'd say take the pressure off by tinkering. That's just a suggestion; feel free to ignore it.

[extract of letter to David Lee]

Bristol, 11.V.2021

I am just finishing a review of Dubuffet and CoBrA, working from books. I'd like to visit the Barbican to see the Dubuffet but I object to the whole mask nonsense. I was considering a visit to London but everything is so stressful and slow at the moment—notwithstanding the reduction in attendance and travel. I'll send the book review along with my tutor's obituary, as well as the Turner Prize analysis.

Re TP, I'm sure Tate thinks of itself as the NHS of British culture—supporting communities through direct action, caring ministration and stewarding the human resources of the nation in the most productive manner. Humans in an ant farm of the maternalistic managerial-elite caste. So, it's not entirely ideological but partly Tate wanting to "do the work". There definitely is an element of hostility towards talented individuals and sympathy with the anonymously staffed collectives. It is sinister—especially because it reveals the anti-humanist mindset of the drones at the Tate. Merit, beauty, aesthetics and connoisseurship have all been decisively and publicly shunned by Tate.

[extract of letter to Dinah Kolka[80]]

Bristol, 24.V.2021

There is a screw in the wall facing my bed and I hang unfinished paintings (canvases) there so that I see them when I am in bed. I can see the picture in good light and half light and it gets me to think about the next alterations. Most of the paintings are landscapes or nudes. The current canvas is of a starving figure lying on the ground. It is part of a series of images relating to colonies, scenes both picturesque and shocking, attractive and repulsive. The group will be painted without explicit artistic commentary. The idea is that the very apparent neutrality is taken as provocative. The one thing an artist is not allowed to be is neutral on the topic of imperialism. It is [a] curious aspect of this image is that the ground takes up a large part of the picture plane and that is purely abstract. The undercoat is black and the upper coat is mixed off-white applied with a palette knife. It was great fun to build that surface. That is the paradox—one can take great enjoyment from painting the most troubling images. One gets caught up in the craft of making without consideration of the subject. Making becomes detached from moral involvement on the part of the maker. I suppose some would consider this situation morally charged. In a recent review, I discussed the corpse

---

80   British-resident Polish author Dinah Kolka wrote for The Mallard at this time.

paintings of Hyman Bloom[81], wherein he painted bodies in spectacular fluorescent colours and unexpected texture. As pure painting, they are entrancing, in terms of motif they are shocking and repellent. I'm sure Bloom considered his corpse paintings to be acts of necessary observance and memento mori and to be a witness of a great truth. I'm also sure Bloom derived great enjoyment (at times) from handling paint and juxtaposing such extravagant colours, notwithstanding the troubling imagery. Do you see an inherent moral contradiction between the pleasure of creation and immoral (or disturbing) subject matter of art? As a creative writer, is there any subject or act you would not depict or refer to solely on moral grounds?

[postcard of Penguin cover of Mantrap to Simon Wilson]

London, 25.I.2023

You missed the inauguration of the dissident art movement last night.[82] A bunch of artists & art lovers have discussed collaboration for months. Forced the issue by announcing it without warning at the discussion panel last night in Camden. We have no options left. We must act. Starved of any public funding, we must seek patrons and crowd funding. I guess we'll put out a manifesto. Already planning a speaking event & an exhibition. Visit to Tate Modern evidence of necessity of action: terrible, vacant, amnesiac art by nobodies collected because of skin colour & reproductive organs & nationality data. Utterly hollow,

---

81   American painter Hyman Bloom (1913-2009) was the subject of the book Erica E. Hirshler, Naomi Slipp, Hyman Bloom: Matters of Life and Death, Museum of Fine Art, Boston, 2019, which Adams reviewed in *The Jackdaw*.
82   See "The Camden Speech".

nothing *there*, a demonstration of elite hegemony stripped of aesthetic content. A power play to humiliate artists & art lovers.

AA

[postcard of Adams's Boy (version C) to JP]

London, 23.III.2023

In London to see space for my July exhibition (Fitzrovia) & review exhibition at a/political gallery, Kennington. Strong exhibition about surveillance & state violence, re Assange, Wikileaks & other topics.[83] "Artivism" but done right—taking on powerful targets & not being dupes. Not sure how much of it is art, but lots to think about. Recommend dropping in. About to review new critical book on [William S. Burroughs]. Will do a litho print in April. Looking forward to making new art.

AA

[letter to Dinah Kolka]

England, 10.IV.2023

Dear Dinah

In preparation for our interview next week (this week), here are some notes. These are for my benefit as much as for yours. Writing helps me clarify my ideas. I shall keep a photocopy.

General

I suppose if we talk about general things I want to achieve with my art, we could say that it involves the transformative

---

83   "States of Violence", a/Political Gallery, London, 24 March–8 April 2023.

shock, catharsis, surprise, the triggering of latent emotions or thoughts due to making unexpected connections. I had this idea about startling the viewer with the "reciprocal image or object". That is, a viewer would encounter something new in art but something that they felt they already knew. The first encounter would provoke *déjà vu*. Often people have said that the image of a painting is familiar to them even though they may never have seen the source. Sometimes it is that sense of recognition and "rightness" that prompts me to select an image (when I use a found image as a source). I suppose part of finding an image is recognising its potency, understanding that is has deep roots in the psyche. That might be a Jungian archetypal legacy imprinted on the cultural unconscious or it might be a personal experience or it could be transvalence—a sort of correlation between an image and a concept or emotion. Sometimes such connections come about in the painting when multiple images come together—two motifs, figure & space, landscape + interior, one composition growing out of (or over) another.

Technique/Approach

That takes us on to how the paintings are made. There are a number of ways: (1) from a single source, found or made by me; (2) from multiple sources, planned or unexpected; (3) from imagination; (4) abstract. When there are sources, I always make changes. Source things excite/engage me; others bore me and they must be reduced in prominence or eliminated. So the paintings are never transcriptions; they are deliberately changed by me during painting. There are also unconscious changes. Very often I get to a point in the painting and I set aside the source. From then on, it is the memory that is important, as well as the logic of the painting. The painting suggests to me how to make itself more complete and effective. The source can be wrong. That is it might have elements that are distracting or detrimental to the painting.

I used to finish a painting in one or two sessions. In the last 20 years I have found working over longer periods makes the paintings richer. I work on multiple paintings at once.

Others

All of this is personal & idiosyncratic, because that is how I found my approach. I am not a theorist. I don't care for theory and don't read it much. Real artists (in my experience) tend not to follow theory. Artists who follow theory or plans tend to lack intuition and intuition is what you need to tell you not just what is a strong image but how to make. You could even say ideas are optional for good art. Fine art isn't a suitable vehicle for especially complex ideas or propositions—not verbal ones. Art operates on a visceral and subconscious level. It has hooks. It compels.

So, I'm not sure how any of this helps other artists. We've formed a group, a movement maybe (we'll see how many people join us and how far we travel together) but I can't see how my approach to art might help them. They might not want advice or example. As soon as say movement gathers, its members start telling others (and themselves) how they were always an outsider and never a true member. All their art is *sui generis* etc.

Routes for the right

I'm not sure I'm of the right, just distinctly not of the left, not a progressive, sceptical of materialism. I see a number of routes for artists of such a temperament. (1) Retvrn to tradition. (2) Reactionary Modernism. (3) Postmodern traditionalism. (4) Vitalism. Of those, I'm strongly in the last camp, with a lot of admiration for reactionary Modernism. By vitalism, I mean holding true to the powerful life energy of truth—of suffering, incompleteness, the urge to find beauty, a recognition of tragedy, understanding eternal cycles and human weakness, using any means necessary to convey insights *directly*. These aspects also deny progress—the permanent impact of materialist change on the human character—and therefore open the door to transcendental experience + knowledge. Vitalism doesn't prescribe a particular style nor necessarily content. It would seem to make adherents wary of hollow forms (1) and also subversion and flippancy (3) but it would permit the artist to use any forms suitable. I shall write more about this in a forthcoming essay, out in time for the July exhibition. I cannot see if our movement will move forwards having one approach, hold different approaches and how the different tendencies will manifest themselves.

The exhibition will be held in central London in early July.[84] We won't be disclosing the location or participants until just before the opening. I shall publish a new pamphlet before then. I will also be making [a] lithograph edition, prints of which will be available for sale this summer. [...]

This might not be any use for your article. Please send me the transcript before publication so I can check and make minimal changes. If I could receive a published version, I would be glad to add it to my archive. You can quote any of this letter in the interview or article.

Shall end letter here. This is already too long.

Best wishes

Alexander

---

84   "The Exhibition", Fitzrovia Gallery, London, July 2023.

[postcard of Brecon and envelope to MK]

Cardiff, 26.IX.2023

Went to Brecon to review exhibition of David Jones's art made near Brecon. Jones was born in Arabin St, Brockley, just around the corner from your flat. We must have walked past his old house (1895-1930s). Great art. Gave me ideas for wood-engravings. [...] Sorry I didn't have a chance to read your manuscript—very busy with books, articles, art. Did you get any agent/publisher interest? My impression is it is tough and that the publishing world is focussed on selling *authors* not stories or even books. It is marketing people who fit demographic targets or who have human-interest back stories. One aspirant novelist friend was shocked & depressed by the agents' websites & realised they wouldn't even read his submission... Heard from established authors that even they can't get worthwhile deals or are being dropped.

A.

[postcard of Guston's Legend to Basil Beattie]

London, 8.X.2023

Powerful, invigorating show of Guston.[85] Some fresh stuff too (Metaphysical paintings & *Fortune* illus.). Great climax of the black paintings. It all starts in 1968 with a horde of *things* rushing in. by 1977-80 we are left with a kettle, a hat, almost nothing. Right to exclude late acrylics—a weak ending, though they aren't bad as paintings. Will review for

85   "Philip Guston Now", Tate Modern, 5 October 2023-25 February 2024.

Jackdaw. Now making money from linocut portraits.
 Best wishes

AA

[extract of letter to KF]

To Bruxelles, 11.X.2023

I am glad that my books, speeches & articles helped you. The aim was to inform, explain, document and advocate; if I met those goals, then I've not wasted anyone's time. I'm sorry that you have to keep secret even your interest in the topics I cover. If only you had more independence from funders who expect political conformity... Setting up alternate economies and career paths is essential for those of us sceptical of the status quo, but I have to appeal to others to fund and network, as I am neither well-connected nor a charismatic leader. You seem to be negotiating the current landscape adeptly.

Bruxelles, 12 + 13.X.2023

A day in Bruxelles, navigating largely from memory. Mont des Arts has become Magritteland, with decals of the man in the bowler hat appearing on large walls. There is a giant apple on top of Musée Magritte. The wondrous apparition is now a readymade publicity icon. I don't blame the museums for doing this, but it wears off something of the magic. I have a particularly strong feeling for Magritte, going back to my early childhood, a line that led me to write my book on his art. I visited Musée Magritte again and found it somewhat reduced (due to loans), with some borrowed pieces I was pleased to see. I missed some of the large bronzes (absent); the shop was closed.
 Also saw a large exhibition of Modernism from (the

country of) Georgia, 1900-1940.[86] It had some impressive pieces but overall it made a stronger case than anticipated. I thought a fair amount of stuff was derivative of French and German art but that's often the case. Lots of new names for me. There were some very striking silent films from the 1920s-1950s. good storytelling, which is often the case with silent cinema. I found the story of the man who neglected his family for alcohol affecting—heavy-handed, of course, but rhetorically fluent. There were stage set models that were absorbing but scale models in space tend to have that quality.

Musée Wiertz was wonderful. I visited it a fair bit when I stayed in the past. Take a look at photographs. It is quite extraordinary. The quality of the art (in terms of design, ideas and emotional tone) is very inconsistent but occasionally wonderful. The building is quite run-down and the Belgians are a little embarrassed by it. Embrace its glorious erratic heroism! If you ever come, make sure to visit. Free entry.

I wandered the narrow medieval streets around Grande Place, full of cafés, souvenir shops, chocolatiers and pubs. (ULB) University students were attending graduation ceremonies in Grande Place, with relatives cheering and applauding from [a] mobile seating stand. In the narrow alleys, foreign waiters solicit customers for ethnic restaurant[s]. visited the museum of ancient art and fin-de-siècle, with superb collection of Renaissance, Mannerist and Baroque art, with Symbolist, Realist and Art Nouveau art & crafts. The collection is huge—seven floors in total. Anyway, you can read my articles if you'd like to know more.

---

86   "The Avant-Garde in Georgia (1900–1936)", Bozar Centre for Fine Arts, Brussels, 5 October 2023-14 January 2024.

How to Start a Dissident Art Movement

[extract of letter to KF]

England, 14.I.2024

The defacement tends to be [of] the clothed figures. I'm not sure why. Maybe it [is] because I see portraits and nudes working in different registers, which consequently sub-consciously changes my imagination chain. As you suggest, perhaps it is related to impressions of clothed power and unclothed vulnerability. I looked a lot at ancient statuary and state portraits, where defacement is the result of de-liberate iconoclasm and testament to the psychological compulsion to conceal identity by assaulting the visage. I wanted to appropriate that impact by replicating the form of defacement. It is quite possible that unconscious impulses direct how I have applied the defacement. What I took from Surrealism was opening oneself up to the power & truth of the emergence of the subconscious through au-tomatic actions and processes, of which this issue seems to be an example. In 1987/1988 I came to fine art (at 14/15) via Surrealism, esp. Magritte.

[letter to OV]

Antwerp, 19-22.III.2024

Dear O.

Came to write review of a Zero Movement abstract paint-er Jef Verheyen.[87] He's very good, although I was slow to warm to him. He gets a bit close to Op Art for my taste, but he was a master technician. In the show were Kleins, Fontanas, Ueckers, Manzonis and so on. Verheyen was an Antwerp painter and died [at] only 54, so this is a big deal

---

87   "Jef Verheyen: Window on Infinity", Royal Museum of Fine Arts, Antwerp, 23 March-18 August 2024.

here. Are you still subscribed to *Jackdaw*? I'll publish my review there.

The museum has some wonderful older paintings. The renovation is largely excellent and sagacious but some interventions I object to because they are frivolous or distracting. Some might even be seen as belittling. There is a seat in a shape of a camel to mimic a camel in a Rubens painting. there is a large fibreglass rock in a room that children can climb in, which resembles a painting of a rock by Patinir. A bronze coffin by Magritte is plonked in front of a pair of Hals portraits. I don't object to lights projecting poems on the floors, nor the painting of a tavern scene hung on a tilt. The proximate hanging of a Basquiat to a Rodin is questionable. Minne next to the Baroque seems better. There was a good Delvaux, nice to see [Jean] Brusselmans in person, a tiny Van Eyck, Fouquet's *Madonna*, some École Saint Martin Laethem. An Ensor solo show. The print room was dark with a central block of walls suspended from the ceiling, glass below and beneath the gallery was visible. Hard to explain in words.

The M HKA (Mus. Cont. Art) had a really strong piece by Viktor Brim—video projections of open-cast mining in Russia & Germany filmed in half-light or night, loud ambient soundtrack.[88] Very little action or movement slow/no panning/zoom. Hypnotic. I don't go for video or installations but this was very effective. I got lost in Lynchian desolate dim planetscapes, industrial architecture, absence of figures, inhuman/indeterminate size.

The other display was Jim Shaw. I didn't find much for me in his art but his collection of thrift-store paintings is astonishing. It became known over in Britain in the '90s. it gave me all sorts of ideas for articles on the overlap between amateur, outsider and folk art. Pin-ups with

---

88   "Beyond the Depths", 20 January-5 May 2024.

roasted chicken skin, acrobats with dislocated anatomies, family snapshots rendered as wild-eyed toothy deformities, cod-Surrealist amalgamations, Hollywood idols transposed to mountain views, naïve self-portraits, symbolic paintings of wrestling avatars, gruesome colour combinations, skew-eyed pet portraits. A veritable cross-section of American consumerism and outsider pathologies. Diagnostic aids to the clinician. They filled the wall of a round room, floor to ceiling. Impressive spectacle. Got me thinking about my square paintings, how they might be best displayed.[89]

Didn't have time to visit the printing museum or pay my respects at Rubens's *Descent from the Cross*. Also, the print museum De Reede was closed during my days here, which is a shame. [...] M HKA had a showing of photos, films and documents related to Gordon Matta-Clark's 1977 project to cut a house located on the main quay of Antwerp, his last big project before he died. Always had a soft spot for him, ever since autumn 1992, when I scoured Goldsmiths Library for books on him. The film showed him working, along with an interview (audio only). Fascinated to watch him cut boards, planks, plaster, beams, concrete, tarpaper, even glass. He was working in such an improvised way— although the drawings on the walls and floors were very calculated—that it was marvellous to watch. One couldn't do it today, nor allow the public near the cut buildings; health-&-safety legislation would prohibit such activities. (He once drove a pick-up truck into the elevated blade of a bulldozer—half [Robert] Smithson happening, half *Jackass* stunt.) I'd like to write about him but without experience of his main sculpture-drawings-cuttings, I can't think of what new I could contribute.

89   See "Bad Painting, Folk Art and Localism".

*[postcard of Wiertz's Greeks and Trojans Fighting
for the Body of Patrocles to Michael Sandle]*

Bruxelles, 28.VI.2024

This is a strangely compelling piece, crackling with hysterical energy and hyper-masculinity. Very large. Wiertz is one of my favourite "bad" artists who's occasionally very impressive. Came to Bruxelles to deliver a speech against traditionalism & Post-Modern/Progressive art to today. Good response. Working towards Harrogate group show, full of confidence despite (because of?) collector indifference. I shall shape the world around me rather than compromise.

   Best regards

                                   Alexander A.

[letter to Rachel Haywire[90]]

England, 14.X.2024

Dear Rachel

As you've been so partial to the square paintings, I thought I'd write you a little about how they came into existence. By 2000 I was 5 years out of art college and felt myself growing more distant from my artist peers, becoming overtaken by lassitude and cynicism. In a fit [of] mischievous bad humour I took up a pornographic magazine, selected a photograph and painted it. I had been thinking of doing something with the images—some project. What caught my eye was the amateur photographs. I was fascinated by all the aspects that an educated maker is taught is gauche—the bad composition, Dutch angles, blurriness, lack of focus, harsh flash light. Further, the graphic bars over the

90   American author and performance artist Rachel Haywire founded the National Futurist Party and Fiume Gallery, New York.

eyes and the unremitting format of the layout seemed unsympathetic. I became absorbed by the clutter—the rug tassels tangled, rumpled sheets, full ashtrays, mismatching underwear discarded, socks drying on a radiator, clamshell mobile phones on grubby carpet. This was social realism without a hint of redemption or improvement nor was [it] a celebration of squalor—it just was what it was, without apology, without introspection. It turned out pretty brutal but I didn't see that at the time.

I just painted. I did women and men in all states of un-dress—fat ones, thin, scrawny, youthful and old, the pretty alongside the repulsive. I just liked recording it as art, like a camera. I filled a studio wall with the paintings all at 16" by 16". It was visible from an upper window and one day an artist came to my studio and said he liked my art and that maybe I would like to see what he was making. He was wearing fluorescent green trainers. I never visited his studio and took down my paintings.

The photographs that worked best for me were from contact magazines. They were magazines where people could send in their photographs and advertise for sex partners. So, for each submission there would be a photo-graph, an area reference and a description for the subject and what they required in a partner(s). It seemed like a cross-section of society and an insight into their private lives—a secret cause of perverse delight and potential ruin. As I worked on the painting series, I found echoes of fine art photography, erotica, ancient statuary, Renaissance painting, Degas canvases and so on all there unknowingly breaking through like an avatar under a thin membrane, an eternal core underlying the ephemeral. That understand-ing came about and took over the pleasure in recording the detritus of daily life.

There didn't seem much future in it. I couldn't exhibit or sell the pictures. I just made them for myself. In 2003 I quit my office job and came up with the idea of selling commissioned paintings, made to order. My friend and I would set up a service where customers could submit photographs to be painted anonymously. We'd even get my friend's girlfriend to offer to take polaroids as part of the scheme. The finished paintings would be delivered wrapped in brown paper and sealed with sealing wax. We'd call it The Naked Spur. I worked on the series, which could be used to provide samples, getting broker by the week. Problem after problem intervened. I got more desperate, accelerating towards poverty and homelessness, surrounded by half a hundred paintings of genitalia, thinking that this would be the day to kill me or make me an underground sensation. The project fell apart and the Naked Spur packed his paintings into crates and left London, never to return.[91]

Years later I painted more pictures from Spanish and German contact magazines—some beautiful things—I still remember the lustre of the polished wooden armrest under the flabby thigh of some half-cropped pallid German woman. The only time any of the paintings were exhibited was in Berlin; just a few were put into a solo show of nudes. We set up a box in the gallery and invited people to anonymously submit photographs and we got a few. I made a lovely painting of a girl's back in the shower.[92] I have no idea who she was. She saw the painting and liked it, mentioning that to the gallerist. Another subject was a middle-aged man who gave an image of himself in a dressing gown, apparently with a cushion in the background printed with his own face. Well, as I wrote, this was in Berlin...

It would be incredible for these ridiculous, wonderful, daring, contrarian, nasty paintings to finally reach an au-

---

91   This was the basis for the novel *The Naked Spur*, written in 2007, published in May 2025.
92   Used as the cover image for *The Naked Spur*.

dience in New York in 2025—a full quarter century after a fit of pique, my perverse desire to make masterpieces that could not be shown[,] budded like one of Baudelaire's *fleurs du mal*.

Yours ever

A.

[extract of letter to Ryan Daffurn[93]]

England, 2.XI.2024

Again, I'd like to say how much I enjoyed inhabiting your world while I was writing the essay. It was refreshing to see your world through your eyes and to be able to transmit that to others, in however a diluted form it might be. Although I see my future as an artist not a writer, it is an important & necessary responsibility to support & promote fellow artists and art one appreciates. In that respect, writing the piece about your art was an important step for me. For many years I reject the idea of writing about living artists, eschewing both praise & criticism, as I thought it was insufficiently distant to allow impartiality. But, what is impartiality other than fear or weakness? Real artists living today need both praise and censure, if intelligent and articulate. I've needed it myself, so denying it to others is unfair. If I can help your art be known more widely, appreciated more deeply and valued more highly then it's my duty—regardless of it also being a pleasure—to do my part.

---

93   Australian painter Ryan Daffurn (b. 1983), about whose work Adams wrote a catalogue essay in 2024.

[letter to Rachel Haywire]

England, 4.XI.2024

Dear Rachel

Perhaps a little more background will show where the square paintings came from. While I was a student at Goldsmiths I had to (unknowingly) overcome an Old Master complex. I was copying Poussin and Titian. I spent (or wasted) my first two years on that then realised (ahead of my third and final year) that I was doing nothing much of worth. (Gaining skills is never entirely without worth.) I embarked on some work that needed quite complex thought and organisation, but was undoubtedly Post-Modernist. But I screwed that up and my tutor (Lisa Milroy) essentially told me this is a mess, it lacks consistency. In frustration—and essentially because I had no other ideas—I started to paint the same image again and again and again, using the same colours, same format, same approach. It was a stab at stability and an attempt to prove consistency. I was going to give my critics consistency of the highest order, even if it alienated everyone. It was an act of stubbornness; I wanted to see how much boredom I could endure. Then I showed the paintings as a block. It actually worked brilliantly. The problem had been resolved by stubbornness, cussedness, a determination to overturn intellect with brute force.

I've pondered what I learned from that experience. Sometimes I think I learned nothing or maybe the wrong lessons. Obsession is necessary and to be a significant artist, you have to be obsessed by materials and objects and images—but not ideas per se. You also need to forget you have an audience. When I was painting the heads at college, I forgot it was an act of defiance. It became a challenge that was private. It was a struggle for my soul. Ony when I surmounted my assumptions that real art came from intellect and homage and fine feelings—and discovered it came from obsession, defiance, boredom and less-than-fine feelings—was I able to make anything worth looking at, yet that happened precisely when I had NO audience. Now I remember what it was like to paint the square nudes, I remember how alone I was. There was no audience for these pictures, no dealers, no buyers, no collectors. Sure, I knew of artists who had made explicit art before, but they were already established artists with dealers and reviews in *Frieze* and *Art Forum*. I was some unknown artist without a proper gallery, working in a tiny studio, with no collectors and no supporters, making art that was seedy and grotesque. I don't say that art has to be private, just that maybe the best of it is made so. I shan't believe there really is any audience until I see the paintings on a gallery wall in NYC. The whole universe seemed to be aligned to prevent these little fragments of sordid reality reaching the eyes of art people. The fact that these images are a mirror to our nature (compromised, versatile, perverted, tender, vulnerable) counts against them being shown well.

To get back to my point. The best work I make with no expectation of an audience or any prospect of sympathy or reward. I'm just "in the zone", operating on instinct, like a marksman or athlete, without conscious calculation. That was true of the heads and of the square nudes. And as I haven't truly accepted that the paintings will reach an audience anywhere—airplanes crashing, consignments going astray, gallery folding, one of us winking out of existence—I will go on thinking that way until I am standing in Fiume Gallery, New York in front of square paintings. Not a minute before that moment will I believe there is an audience for the square paintings. I'll paint in that spirit until that day.

Yours ever

A.

[extract of letter to Simon Wilson]

England, 16.I.2025

News today of the death of David Lynch. I shall write something about him. I respected his work a lot. He was a true artist as a director, as well as being an accomplished visual artist. Thinking about him as a pursuer of beauty, a man unafraid of becoming obsessed by what excited him. Real artists are possessed by what draws them; they don't dabble. Sometimes very simple things take one. Ideas or images can be quite obvious but they exert a hold over even flexible, adroit artists who are in command of their mediums—their metiers. Lynch was one of those. I saw a lot of Bacon—and something of [William] Burroughs—in Lynch.

[letter to Martina Markota[94]]

England, 17.IV.2025

Dear Martina

Thank you for agreeing to read *The Naked Spur* next month. In advance I have sent you *Noctes*, which reproduces some of the square paintings that are at the core of the *TNS* narrative. This should help you to understand the character of the paintings that the protagonist makes in the novel. [...]

As much in *Noctes* is strange, ugly and obscene as there is that is beautiful, beguiling and tender. It was always meant to be so. I wanted the ugly alongside the beautiful, old with the young, black, white, Asian, etc. It would be a cross-section of humanity detached from taste or aesthetics (artistic and anatomical). Some of the pictures I find very beautiful but many are not—just odd, some grotesque. The

94   American burlesque performer, author and photographer Martina Markota.

addition of the basins, objects and room corners was in order to act as punctuation, to make the stream of bodies less overwhelming. The oddness of seeing a basin or object had its own power and compulsion. When I compiled the book the intention was not just to record the square painting series but to construct something powerful and disconcerting, as if *Noctes* were the scrapbook of a serial killer. When you see these images, you think that these are forbidden or private or confidential—contraband that is potentially dangerous (injurious) to your wellbeing or could make you criminally implicated in some squalid transgression. *Noctes* was intended as an artistic experience that would be troubling and lead the reader-viewer to wonder about the sanity and intentions of the maker. That was also my intention when writing *TNS*. The reader should worry about what he/she is observing; they should be absorbed by a protagonist who immerses himself in a world of indulgence and be concerned for themselves, being numbed by extreme imagery and hedonistic excess. The inclusion of the most obscene and absurd images is done to remind people of how extreme the material is, to prevent them becoming fully entranced by the attractive or exciting. There are some images that are just too discomforting to be processed and normalised through repeated consumption.

This will all become a lot more comprehensible when the novel reaches you. Most readers of the novel will never see these paintings—indeed, I don't think any of these paintings have ever been exhibited and they may never be—but you'll get to understand the protagonist's actions and outlook better through having seen *Noctes*.

Best wishes

Alexander

[letter to Martina Markota]

England, 19.IV.2025

Dear Martina

I hope you'll forgive my previous letter & enclosure. It is a great relief to communicate with fellow artists, especially when you feel you can share your best work. I'm not sure if *Noctes* is what I'll be remembered for—if I'm remembered at all—but it was the time when I was most brave, most reckless. Only recently have I regained that fire, that desire to prove myself. The gallery project with Rachel gave me a boost with the possible prospect of an audience in NYC for my paintings (my square nudes—my boldest pieces), the impending publication of *The Naked Spur* and the forthcoming exhibition in Warsaw all energise me. Communicating with artists who are on a similar wavelength also pushes me really to raise my game. *The Naked Spur* is partially about the way artists can drift [when] they become separated from colleagues. Man is a social animal and the artist cannot thrive as an atomised individual, because he embodies the human spirit. It reminds me of Nietzsche's conception of the artist as lawgiver & leader. One can't fulfil that role in isolation. It can be lonely to make difficult art but it can also be an excuse for retreat when an artist *seeks rejection*. When the artist abandons his calling and shuns society, he embraces the liberal misconception of human nature and the fallacy of the lone genius; that is often just cowardice and turning away from the serious artist's role as leader, lawgiver, shaman. In the novel, the protagonist turns his back on friends, colleagues, partners and foregoes his duties. He forces those around him to reject him and his art. It's a story exposing nihilism—disillusion with the lies he's swallowed—I'm ready to see that message published now

I'm a stronger man who won't shirk his destiny.
    Best regards

Alexander

[letter to Ryan Daffurn]

England, 25.IV.2025

Dear Ryan

I wonder about how much to write on the topic of my political-intellectual development. I'm not amenable much to theory and I'm not an artist driven by intellect and abstract ideas. I don't want to misrepresent myself or assume airs. However, as these issues have been on my mind, it would be disingenuous to neglect them entirely. Previously, I've thought anything I cannot explain well and [don't] have a fairly clear understanding of I should not make public. As part of my growth, it seems like it would be beneficial to map out how my thoughts on art have changed. The conclusions are less important than the act of consideration. That's one reason I continue to write reviews and articles, aside from the functions of giving information and improving morale. Reviewing exhibitions really helps me to order my thoughts, compare my ideas to reality and encounter art that could spark my own art. For example, it was seeing David Jones's wood-engravings that inspired me [to] take up the medium. I'm starting my first engravings in a couple of weeks, whenever the blocks arrive. Seeing the art of others always enlightens me about my own art. Writing about your paintings allowed me to rank and assess what counted for me in art, including the work I have done.

Happily, because of the type of artist I am and my outlook on art, I've never fallen into the trap of intellectualising art or relying on theory. I've tended to have a Formalist attitude, reading the qualities of plastic art found in it. I was immunised against Conceptualism while at college. Seeing the nonsense Conceptualism produced was enough inoculation. Plus all the excuses that came out in tutorials & convenor groups, those were so tortuous and transparent that a bunch of us in my course were strongly averse to resting upon structures of ideas, even our own. For us, we'd pull stuff apart in private conversations, just shred the work but pull out parts we liked, the aspects we responded to. It was a way of testing what we understood, what we thought art should do. I am sure it made us feel authentic artists by arguing over Ryman, Rothko, Kline and poking fun at the hipsters with their neurotic craft. That must have imprinted itself on me. A lot of what I've said and written is derived from the canon (Gr: measuring stick) and the attitudes I formed back in the studio at college. I have changed some of my judgments (accepting the value of decoration, for example) and I am more open to contrary approaches, but much of the way I frame things came from Goldsmiths and even Wrexham, where I was before. My tutors and the students I clicked with, we had no patience with nonsense and pretension however our tastes and output differed. The problem is that this doesn't always translate between cultures. The art students of German art schools didn't really get my attitude and I realised I was better off not getting involved in direct debate in the way I used to in Britain. I got people upset and alienated whereas in London people could shrug it off or laugh or simply take a different perspective and leave it at that. And I wasn't on any sort of crusade to win followers. Under such circumstances you're better off desisting. How did you find things in Leipzig? What was your experience of talking art with students from German art schools? Do you think Australian schools take after what I've told you about my set in Goldsmiths or theorycels (as we call them now) or the deferential credentialist approach of the

Germans? I was always rather amused by the way German artists would go on putting their professor's name in their CV even 10 or 20 years out of Kunstschule. I just dismissed it as credentialism but if you have more of an atelier system then using the name of a master has some evidential value in establishing a lineage. Me, I don't care much for that. It might go into a book but I'd never put it on the wall of an exhibition.

Anyway, that's enough. Write when you can and when you feel like it.

As ever

A.

[letter to CH]

England, 25.IV.2025

Dear C——

Working on two difficult essays for a book which should appear at the end of the year. The first is reconsidering my stance of 2016-8 against identity politics. The second is about breaking the hold liberalism has over us. I write about drowning the idols of egalitarianism, democracy, equality, multiculturalism and materialism. The two pieces will be very controversial, that is why I am holding them back for the book. Want to have something strong & fresh for buyers. The logic of rejecting liberalism—seeing its true face, its squalid origins, its appalling consequences, its awful future—entails confronting the implications of that rejection. That will be tackled in two ways. First will be a recognition that art is an expression of cultural hegemo-ny—as the Marxists say—and a recognition of the power of collection action and why dissenters must be prepared to accept and adapt following that admission. The second part will urge artists to be vigilant against old beliefs and their progressive education rising up to confuse them. The second piece is called "Drown Everything", which is likely the name of the book.

I know that a lot of artists won't go along with me. Curious to see at what point acquaintances drop out, where their limits are. The first 4 books are essentially the product of a disillusioned liberal. This next will be something a lot stranger & stronger. It won't be the end. I'm still learning. My education has been so slow. I'm catching up, re-reading stuff I didn't properly understand at college and reading new material (old books—Evola, Nietzsche, Hamsun, Spengler). Once you start to drown the idols of your official education (ideals not authors), suddenly new horizons unfurl like a roll of virgin canvas. I'm not a good or eloquent exponent of the ideas themselves but I feel they do me good & help me see the vain platitudes of what I previously took (somewhat unthinkingly) as wisdom.

This doesn't affect much what I look at and respond to in art nor how I make art. It may not make my art better. Let's hope it doesn't make it inferior. I don't repudiate any of my old art, something that will become a matter that I will probably be questioned about in a series of events and interviews over May and June. The timing is not great as it coincides with the Warsaw exhibition opening 6.VI. I like the adrenalin kick of interviews & openings but the comedown is grinding and it gets in the way of *making*, which is at the heart of what excites me as an artist. There will be at least four interviews & a launch. The reviews are not my business, but somehow they take up my time (to circulate and reply to—I mean thank not rebut). When will I be able to immerse myself in the page, canvas or wood block?

Please let me know how your projects are faring. Forgive this scrawl.

Best wishes

A.

How to Start a Dissident Art Movement

[letter to OV]

England, 28.IV.2025

Dear O.

I've been thinking about the texts that inspired me when I was young (and since then). I mean texts about art. I thought of Van Gogh's letters, Delacroix's journal, Bacon's interviews, Greenberg's reviews and articles, Wyndham Lewis's reviews, Hulme's pieces on Modernism. There's also some value in Sickert's articles [and] Serra's writings & interviews. Bowden's speeches on reactionary Modernism are energising. Some letters by Magritte are very good but the interviews much less so. Manifestoes leave me cold, more or less. Judd and Motherwell can be good but apart from Judd's famous essay ("Specific Objects"?[95]), I can't remember being excited by either of them. Most often art helps, but life is better—a scene, experience, image, person. Can you think of texts that inspired you? What did we talk about in the studio? What [are] the qualities in a text that fill one with hope as a maker of art? Insight, good judgment, confident assertions, stable principles, clear writing, directness, belief in art (and the culture that produces it). It helps if one trusts the author as an artist, but Greenberg and Sylvester are great writers without being artists. By and large, theorists are never compelling, even if they might produce viable ideas. I don't know if rhetoric enters into it. I'm sure advocacy does—advocacy of someone's art or one's own ideas, experience or output. Any thoughts?

Who could we read today? Who speaks to serious artists? Maybe my problem is that I don't visit exhibitions of new art, so I never encounter new art reviews. I suppose

---

95   Judd's article "Specific Objects" was published in 1965 and became a seminal text for Minimalism.

when identity is the only criterion, there isn't much you can write about the art. You can't critique the art because that is tantamount to criticising the identity. Therefore, all critical apparatus is redundant, only political advocacy remains. [...]

Well, there isn't much else to add. Again, thanks for the meeting. It was a great boost. Oh, regarding our discussion about the pitfalls of trad, I will likely write a follow-up piece distinguishing "trad" from "traditional". That is, "trad" being a lifestyle choice—a skin suit worn by materialists & progressives, actually discrediting tradition—and tradition being a continuity of spirit and values. My first piece concentrated on trad v Mod./P.Mod. There is more to add.

Best wishes

A.

[letter to Michael Sandle]

England, 6.V.2025

Dear Michael

Thanks for your consent regarding my letters.

I was sorry to hear of your travails. I hope you recover soon & keep your spirits up. Working is essential for us artists. I know you're not a religious man but I'm sure I am right to detect in you a powerful, unquenchable belief in your destiny to make great art. It is your fate. Ultimately, great artists do not choose their fates; they accept their destinies and fulfil their callings with alacrity, with majesty, with unequivocating commitment. You have. Few artists are blessed to be so touched by ferocious tenacity and great ambition and wonderful talent as you are, Michael. So, considering, how can you not work for as long as possible? I can't see a better way of employing your remaining time. I feel that too, though with less compulsion. I do one thing well—making art—it would be a reckless dereliction of my calling to do anything else.

So, yes, setting aside appearances, interviews, exhibitions, etc. in favour of creating is not just the wisest choice, it is the *only* viable choice. I shall write again once I've sent off my large canvases to Warsaw.

Best regards

Alexander

The launch of my novel will be in Hoxton, evening of 28 May. Quite understand if you pass.

[extract of letter to Rachel Haywire]

England, 15.V.2025

I know what your interlocutor meant. It is the very awkwardness of the square paintings that is their hallmark. The blend (between works, as well within) runs the gamut of the beautiful to the ugly, classic to scuzzy, familiar to bizarre, tender to repellent. And, as I said, get your newly appointed head of art sales to talk about the zone of uncertainty in the art. It's the product of a liminal artist, the member of the excess elite, disenfranchised, working as an outsider, a dissident faction of a single individual (at war with himself). "I AM A CELL OF ONE." The isolated artist as ersatz criminal, a lone wolf at once highly romantic + idealistic + also vain, deluded, selfish. The attempt to demolish the art world with a seedy sexy picture, parallelling Cézanne's attempt to "conquer Paris w/ an apple". I will write about this parallel between criminal & artist in an article called "I am a cell of one", based on a phrase of B.S. Johnson.[96] Artist + criminal as men of action... notorious figures both lionised + scorned... abnormally high in disagreeableness.

96   See "Vir Heroicus Sublimis", original publication title "I am a Cell of One".

Criminals are rarely excess elites (excluded from Pareto's circulation of the elite) but artists sometimes are. I didn't make this very obvious in *The Naked Spur* because it was written before I studied elite theory, but I think it bears being drawn out. [...] The artist as an endurance performer willing to risk everything on a mad scheme designed to show up the limitations of the art world is an accurate picture. (*Irony*: everyone in the art system already knows it's a fake; that single rebel artist is the dummy who caught on late and thinks he's noticed something new.) At the heart of it is powerful art that gets under your skin, regardless of the artist's motivation.

[extract of letter to CH]

England, 16.V.2025

I should tell you that this novel is about 90% accurate to my experience, 10% invented. It is up to you to choose which 10% you think I concocted and apply that to the 10% you consider most deplorable. All the art described exists. It is contained in the textless book *Noctes*.

[extract of letter to Piotr Bernatowicz[97]]

England, 16.V.2025

I am really proud of the work I've made for our exhibition. It connects very closely with the pieces I've made in the past. Thus the Warsaw paintings, drawings and prints are an extension of the art made about Berlin. The tragedy of war is a burden carried by the nations of the combatants—including the servicemen and the civilians and

97   Polish curator, author, museum director and gallerist Piotr Bernatowicz (b. 1973) founded his gallery S7, Warsaw in late 2024 and invited Adams to exhibit there.

apparent in the legacy of physical culture (the buildings, art, artefacts, landscape)—not always equally, but always shared. "Kinderszenen" is a chance for Poles to see facets of their social history refracted through a foreign artist's perspective. I trust they will evaluate the display fairly and thoughtfully. You have given me a wonderful opportunity, for which I thank you, Piotr.

[postcard of Adams's Boy (version C) to Michael Sandle]

England, 21.V.2025

Dear Michael

I'm going to write an article recommending that a statue/memorial to victims of the Barbary slave raids be erected in Britain. Hew Locke gets £1,000s to wrap up statues of others in the name of decolonialism but not £5 goes from the public purse to a monument to countless men, women & children brutalised & abducted.[98] (Maybe one can go up for the Irish deported to the American colonies.) You should design it. It could be the culmination of your lifetime's critique of systemic barbarity/inhumanity.

Best

AA

98   British sculptor Hew Locke (b. 1959) won numerous commissions by public bodies to produce installations relating to the Atlantic African slave trade.

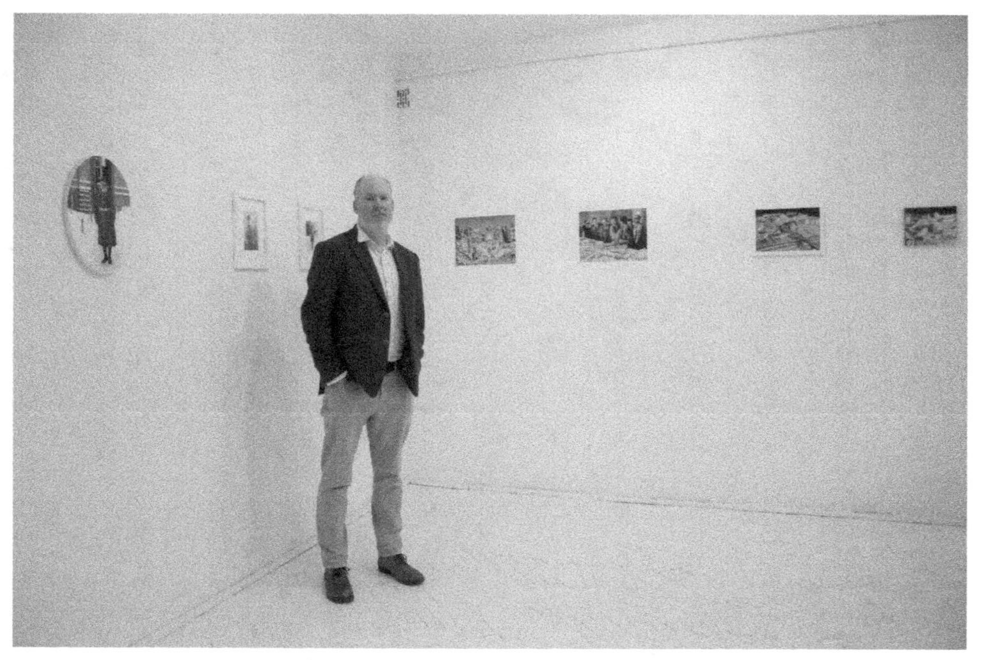

AA at "Kinderszenen", S7 Gallery, Warsaw, 7 June 2025

[postcard of St George's Hall, Liverpool to Simon Wilson]

Warsaw, 7.VI.2025

Travelled via Liverpool to Warsaw for "Alexander Adams: Kinderszenen", an exhibition mainly of new paintings.[99] Two large canvases delayed in delivery but we were able to hang a strong display. Based on Polish history 1900-1947. Got beautiful afternoon sunlight in one room. Poles reacted well to the art & subjects. Great poster. Despite the absence of the centrepieces, it is a strong exhibition. The 2 large paintings I shall hang in July for an Old Town festival. Warm response from audience heartens me. Waiting for full considerations to *The Naked Spur* in press and personal.
   Regards

A.

[extract of letter to Fen de Villiers[100]]

Warsaw, 7.VI.2025

The gallery is S7. The director founded it after taking inspiration from my article on next steps for the movement.[101] The momentum is heading our way. From my conversations here it seems (in Poland at least) artists, curators and collectors understand that state institutions are hollowed out—zombie organisations—and that our future is in building networks independently so that they are resilient to change. Even those on the right who thought that hold-

---

99   "Alexander Adams: Kinderszenen", S7 Gallery, Warsaw, 6 June-20 July 2025.
100   British sculptor Fen de Villiers (b. 1989) studied and lives in Antwerp. He and Adams exhibited together in "The Exhibition", Fitzrovia Gallery, London, July 2023.
101   See "Components of an Art Movement".

ing government would see them through have witnessed their efforts overturned. All except the oldest and most stubborn see the future of any vital culture springs from independent networks, with the state promoting & acquiring the fruits of that scene retrospectively. The scene itself can't be germinated, nurtured or sustained by state funding. The folly of central funding is obvious from the Polish experience (speaking from a dissident view point). Elites in art are not synonymous with state organisations—especially not a counter-elite high culture. Plenty of lessons to be drawn here.

[extract of letter to PL]

England, 30.VI.2025

I'm making a painting for the cover of my next book. It is called *Argonaut* and has a nude man standing, facing towards a flat plain, mountains beyond and cloudy sky above. It is a manifesto painting—symbolic first and foremost. I really admire Beckmann and so this is a homage to him but I will dedicate it to my uncle, who is dying in Spain at the moment. He's in his final days or weeks and he faces this journey—to die well. I remember reading the *Tibetan Book of the Dead* when I was young—the various stages & places the man would encounter. The painting is a manifesto in that it is setting out the challenges a thinking person must endure. The effort, monotony, stamina, courage, ingenuity and so forth that any brave informed person must experience (and summon up) when they choose to go beyond cossetted deracinated life, that is the real subject of the painting. I can't say I've conquered anything but I do see much of the terrain ahead. I'm only starting out.

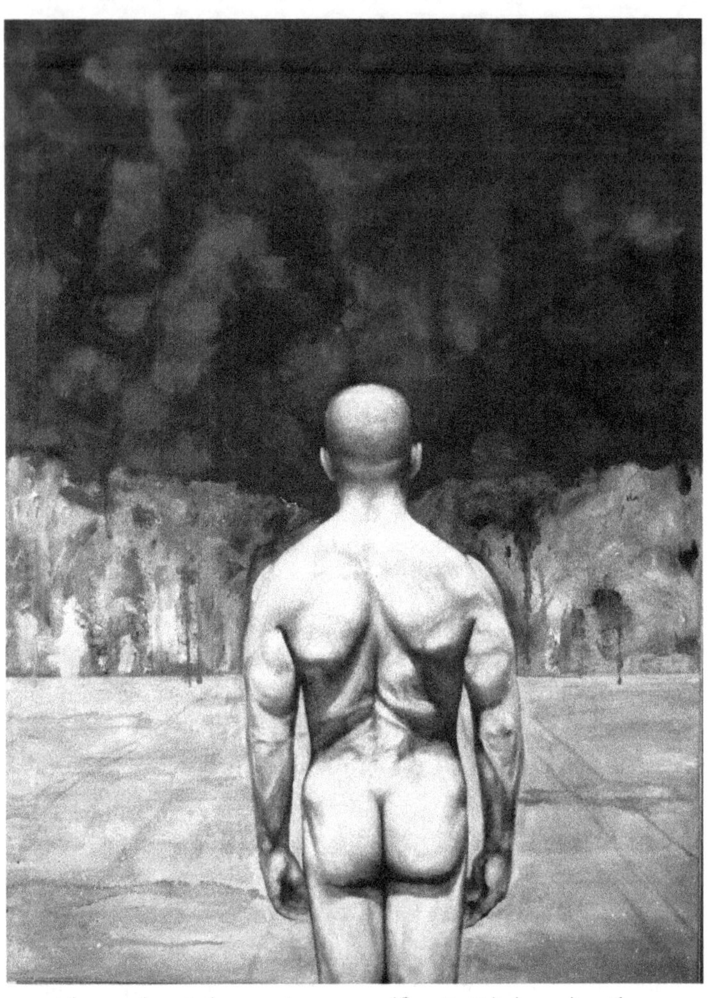

Alexander Adams, *Argonaut* (for R.C.) (2025), oil on
canvas, 36" x 26"/91 x 66 cm

CHRONOLOGY OF THE AUTHOR

1973	Born in London
1973-85	Living in Berkshire
1986	Moves to North Wales
1991-2	Studies fine art at Wrexham College of Art, North Wales
1992-5	Studies BA Fine Art/History of Art at Goldsmiths College, London, under Roger Bates, Lisa Milroy and Basil Beattie
1992-2003	Living mainly in London
2003	Extended visit to Spain (May-Nov.)
2003-5	Living in North Wales
2005-6	Living in Newcastle-upon-Tyne
2007-14	Living in Berlin, with numerous visits to Belgium
2007	Begins regularly publishing articles and reviews on art and literature
2011	Publication of first volume of poetry (Jun.). Artist-in-residence, Albers Foundation, Connecticut (Sep.-Dec.).

2014-5   Living in Cardiff

2015-22   Living in Bristol

2018   Awarded Artist Scholarship by the Francis
           Bacon Art MB Foundation, Monaco (Jan.).
           Delivers first cultural-political speech, at the
           Barbican Centre, London (Oct.).

2019   Publishes *Culture War: Art, Identity Politics
           & Cultural Entryism*, first book on cultural
           politics (Mar.)

2022   Recommences printmaking. Moves to
           Northern England (Nov.).

2023   Marries Amy Adams

2025   Publication of *The Naked Spur*, first novel
           (written 2007) (May)

TEXTUAL HISTORY

"Introduction", "The Barbican Speech" and "The Camden Speech" all unpublished; "The New Impressionists" or "How to Start an Art Movement" published on the Substack account of Alexander Adams (www.alexanderadamsart.substack.com), 28 January 2023; "Towards a Based Barbican" published as a pamphlet by Golconda Fine Art Books, March 2022; "High Risk, High Reward: The Reactionary Temperament in the Arts" published as "Dealers & Gamblers" in *IM-1776*, 14 February 2023; "Components of an Art Movement" published on Substack, 1 August 2023; "The Coventry Speech" unpublished; "I'm no Old Master, nor are you" published on Substack, 26 August 2023; "Bad Painting, Folk Art and Localism" published on Substack, 14 May 2024; "The Future is not Trad" published on Substack, 21 April 2025 (postscript unpublished); "*Vir Heroicus Sublimis*" published as "I am a Cell of One" on Substack, 17 May 2025; part II only of "Green Suns & Cyber-Cathedrals: On National Futurism" published as "On National Futurism" on Substack, 10 July 2025; "Art as Attrition" published in *The Jackdaw*, July/August 2025, pp. 12-3; "Twelve Rules for Artists", "Drown Everything", "Letters" and "Chronology" all unpublished. Some texts were shortened for their first publication; the versions published here are the full original texts.